A Soul's Journey

Other Titles From New Falcon Publications

A Soul's Journey

Whispers From The Light

Patricia Idol

NEW FALCON PUBLICATIONS
TEMPE, ARIZONA, U.S.A.

Copyright © 1996 by Patricia Idol

International Standard Book Number: 1-56184-098-X

First Edition 1996

Cover Art by Denise Cuttitta

The paper used in this publication meets the minimum requirements of the American National Standard for Permanence of Paper for Printed Library Materials Z39.48-1984

Address all inquiries to:
NEW FALCON PUBLICATIONS
1739 East Broadway Road Suite 1-277
Tempe, AZ 85282 U.S.A.
(or)
1209 South Casino Center
Las Vegas, NV 89104 U.S.A.

"An oyster
accepts his pain
and
makes of it
a pearl."

TO MY FAMILY

To Charlie, who unconditionally loved and patiently put up with me for thirty-seven years.

To Chris, my first born, who tirelessly waded through draft after draft of this book, correcting my grammar and my atrocious spelling.

To Jennifer, my littlest angel, who considered it a forgone conclusion that this book would be published.

To Janet and Marion, my daughters-in-law, for honoring me with their friendship and love.

To David Shane, Matthew Shane, and Stephen Christopher, my grandsons, who along with their future brothers, sisters, and cousins shall carry the light into the next generation.

To Shane and Michelle whose love turned my face toward the light.

Thank you all for the joy that loving you has brought to my life. Your unconditional love, endless patience, constant encouragement, and unflinching faith has helped to make this book a reality.

TABLE OF CONTENTS

Introduction

Our Master said, "You shall know the truth and the truth shall set you free." He did not explain what truth, nor from what you would be freed. Those speaking to me through the channels of my mind express their knowledge as the truth and something deep within the recesses of my soul knows that it is so. I can neither prove, nor disprove any of what has been conveyed. I must, therefore, depend upon a deep sense of recognition which has resided within my being since I became aware of my conscious thought process and seems to inevitably home in on knowledge of an omnipotent source. I have learned through experience that I can trust its guidance and, in fact, must follow that guidance if I am to experience harmony within my life as it unfolds here. I can no more separate myself from God than I can subsist without breath and nourishment. Listening to the whispers of the Father's voice within my mind, has indeed brought to me an unequivocal sense of knowing and peace. So much so, that upon feeling threatened I immediately seek the only counsel which has proven to be completely loving and reliable.

Since this pattern of communicating with and relying upon that still small voice within had become second nature, it was understandable that when the unthinkable occurred within my life not once, but twice I should turn to it, knowing that I would find within it truth, love, and the strength to cope with whatever befell. At such times it is as if a presence descends upon me, rendering me calm, resilient and able to cope. The sensation is almost ethereal, as if I were standing in the calm eye of a raging storm. The presence always remains until I am able to cope on my own. It loves, protects, and encourages me. I could not, nor do I wish to experience life without it. In 1987, twenty-two months after my son's death, this loving presence gained voice and through the strength and confidence which comes from

11

being completely and unconditionally loved, enabled me to be drawn into the wisdom of its reality.

Those who share their wisdom with me have proven to my satisfaction time after time in various ways that they speak the truth. I know beyond a shadow of a doubt that were these who speak to me not representatives and messengers of the Father, He would have told me and their truths would have turned to dust and vanished.

I understand that the general populace, including the organized church, no longer believes that God speaks to individuals in this manner. This has troubled me somewhat, for this belief closes the door on so many exquisitely beautiful possibilities and opportunities for communion with a love which can not be found within this world. However, I know without reservation that not only has God spoken to me, but through me as well. Just as He speaks to anyone who will listen. I have simply taught myself to listen.

No more perfect being has ever entered the body than the Master, Jesus, the Christ, yet, despite His innate wisdom, love and kindness, He was rejected by many of those with whom He came in contact. If man would not accept and believe Him then how could I ever expect to be taken seriously? When I consulted the wise ones about my doubts, asking how I could possibly expect others to believe that I was God's messenger, they replied very succinctly, "because it is true." They can not understand why we have such difficulty accepting the truth when it is given, nor realizing that they do not engage in flattery or ego building. They are incapable of falsehood.

I must confess that I have gone through periods of doubt from time to time. I have considered every possibility, including the likelihood that it could simply be my imagination. When I voiced this doubt they countered, "And where does imagination originate?" You can not ask questions, nor cast doubts which I, myself, have not entertained.

There is, however, one indisputable shining ray of light which constantly illuminates this whole collection of knowledge. It advocates only love, beauty, peace and light. If, as the Master says, "You may know a tree by its fruit," then certainly this knowledge is the fruit of God's tree. Remember the verse you learned as a child, "God is love"? This dear brothers is the fruit of that tree.

Only love great enough to banish all fear allowed me to follow my son through the door which separates our worlds. Had I not loved him more than I feared the unknown, I would have never had the courage to disregard what was accepted as possible and attain what was believed to be impossible. I have learned to trust something beyond my five senses, that spark of God which resides within us all and involuntarily seeks its own.

I can tell you that never have I felt so loved as when these sent by the Father are present. I have experienced "the peace that passes understanding." My beliefs are no longer limited by any particular dogma, but continue to unfold and expand to include all that is the Father. I know from the depths of my soul that this knowledge is truth and the beings who bring it are unconditionally loving and sent by the omnipotent source of all that is. They have come, offering me love, wisdom, understanding, and peace. I have learned to believe completely in the power of God to transcend logic by using the supernatural or any other means at His command. I trust and believe what He tells me. For those of you who feel I risk the punishment of hell for my beliefs I would reply... I have been there. I chose not to stay. It was there that our Father found me, offered me His hand and led me into the light. In return for all His tender love and care, He made but one request of me, that I share the light with my brothers. So, dear brothers, I share with you in these pages the beauty of that love. It is yours to accept or deny. I offer it with the same loving spirit in which it was offered to me.

What follows represents five years of shared love, communication, faith, trust, and just plain hard work. It has enriched my life in a way which defies description. God and His world of loving beings of light does not exist in some remote netherworld, nor is this promised plane of being a pipe dream. It is a vital, loving, limitless reality. This world in which we reside is not even a pale shadow. This I know! How do I know you ask? If I were to ask you how you know that China exists if you have not seen it, you might reply that someone you trust and whose knowledge you respect had told you. Well, someone I know and trust and whose wisdom I respect has confirmed these truths. I have visited these other realities, as well, just as many of you have without being aware of it. The Father's world is alive, limitless, and as accessible as you wish it to be. The only barrier restricting you is fear and logic. Logic is the lock which imprisons you. I have learned the truth and it has set me free from the fear which separated me from the legacy of my Father.

CHAPTER I

MICHELLE

I cannot possibly tell my story without telling Shane and Michelle's story, since the fact that it happened at all was because I was allowed the privilege of being their mother. With their birth I embarked on an endless journey down a path that would bring about changes in my personality, my way of looking at things, and would completely restructure my belief system. My own private joke is that somewhere among the ethers before I entered this life, when asked what I would like to experience, I must have with my usual impulsiveness piped up, "Oh everything." I haven't missed much. Childhood was extremely difficult for me, due in part to an alcoholic father with a potential for violence and a mother whose means of coping was to silently endure. Because I seemed to have some success at controlling my father when he was drinking, the responsibility of running interference between my parents was delegated to me. Rather than being protected, I was the protector. Once in a childish fit of petulance, I complained about the uneven distribution of responsibility by asking my mother why this duty always fell to me instead of someone else, she replied, "Because you have to learn to be very strong." I don't think, at the time, she had any idea how profound that statement would prove to be.

I was married at the age of eighteen to a strong gentle man who gave me love and patiently set about building a sense of self worth in me. For the first time I felt secure and protected. Ten and one half months after our marriage I gave birth to our first son, a sweet, gentle, precocious little boy who brought the sunshine with him. I was happy and fulfilled. I had always loved children and wanted several.

At the age of twenty one I was again pregnant. Looking back, I realize that from the beginning of the pregnancy there was a persistent sense of foreboding. It was not a feeling I wished to

15

discuss with anyone, for fear that giving it voice might give it substance. I convinced myself that my anxiety was caused by the fact that I did not feel well during most of the pregnancy

Our daughter was born in the early morning hours of Easter Sunday, April 22, 1962. The foreboding had become reality. Eight hours after her birth, our tiny Michelle lost her valiant struggle to live. My education had begun. I don't know that I can explain how excruciatingly painful losing your child is. There is a sense of numb bewildering disbelief, a hope that someone will rush in and tell you a mistake has been made. The moment you are told and the specific words used play incessantly in your head like a needle stuck on a phonograph record. Death makes others apprehensive and awkward. They come tentatively, reminded of how fragile their own existence is and in their feelings of helplessness they resort to platitudes and clichés. You are quietly told that, you are young and can have more children, the important thing is that you are alright. They say, "It's good you didn't have her long enough to become attached, or we are not meant to understand these things, or it's God's will." I cringed at how often I had piously spouted those same platitudes. When one is grieving, no platitude, no matter how well meant, is of any comfort. I was distressed that she seemed to be reduced to the status of a non entity because I was not allowed the privilege of bonding with her. Indeed, I had been bonding with her for the nine months I had carried her beneath my heart. The single most bewildering aspect of the grieving process when one loses an infant is the fact that there are no memories. There are no little endearments and moments of togetherness to look back on, no photographs and keepsakes to weep over. What there is, is a feeling of being cheated and a haunting sense of failure. Having always been afraid to share my deepest feelings with others, I put on a brave face and retreated within where I could examine and lick my wounds privately without having to explain the mounting anger that was beginning to seethe within me. I was angry with those who tried to console me. I think I was angriest with those who told me it was God's will and we are not meant to understand. Deep within I was venting my frustration by angrily asking God all the things I dare not say aloud. I could not understand why He had taken my child. Why did He give with one hand and take back with the other? What had I done that was so terrible that He had to take my child from me?

Grieving is a process which cannot be shared. It is selfish and solitary and affects each individual in his own unique way. I was later to learn that there are stages of grief and I had run the gamut from denial, to anger, to fear of losing the child I had. Life seemed so fragile. The questions constantly nagged and agitated me. I had read the Bible since I had been able to read and was especially fond of the Gospels. I loved and was fascinated by the teachings of Jesus. They spoke of love and a God who loved you so perfectly that He could forgive you anything. He taught that life was eternal and continued after death. He said, "Seek and you shall find; knock and the door shall be opened" (Matt. 7:7-9). Were these things that had been written truth or were they just pipe dreams meant to pacify a fatalistic society? Was there really a heaven? Did the soul occupying the body continue to live on somewhere after death? If so why all the mystery? Why wasn't specific information made available so that one did not have to agonize over the well being of their loved ones. At this point all I wanted to know was that somewhere the soul which was my child lived and was loved and nurtured. Who comforted her if she was frightened or lost? Who loved and protected her?

I had been raised in an era of "hell fire and damnation" religion which painted very graphic pictures of heaven and hell with no grey areas. The good went to heaven, the bad went to hell. What of this tiny girl who had not been within this world long enough to be either? Why was death visited upon the young without allowing them the opportunity to realize their potential?

"Dear God, do you love us and if you do why do you inflict such agony?" I had no idea where to go for answers. There had never been anyone in my life that I had talked to, not about what I really felt and thought. Growing up in the 40's and 50's, dissenting questions about established religious doctrine were not even spoken of in whispers. You simply did not question God. The only one who had ever seen inside me was God and I wasn't even sure of Him anymore. Maybe "they" were right. Maybe this was my punishment for even thinking the questions. I did not, at that time, understand the difference between religion and spirituality. I was slowly by degrees drowning in my own despair and there was no one else who could answer my questions, no one who could understand my need to know. I begged and pleaded with God to help me to understand. Funny, it did not occur to me that He would refuse to answer. "Seek and you shall find," He had said, "Knock and the door shall be opened."

OK, I knocked, not in anger, but as a hurt bewildered child asking of a loving parent what I had done that was so terrible.

It is interesting the people and events we draw to ourselves to teach us the lessons we need to learn. This was a truth I did not yet comprehend and would not for sometime yet. Looking back, it's almost as if it happened to someone else. In a sense that is an accurate statement since I am no longer the person I was when I was 22. At that time I did not believe there could be any worse pain than I had already endured. Dear God, how very young and naive I was. With the gift of hind sight I see that God had a definite pattern of offering me understanding over the years. A pattern which began about this time.

I hesitate to call myself a religious person, for the connotation implies a stuffy, pious, holier than thou superiority that I have never wanted to portray. I have for most of my life, however, had ongoing conversations with God in my mind. For me it was a natural process and nothing out of the ordinary.

Nonetheless, the fact that hearing voices had for centuries been cause to question one's sanity and had created many a religious pariah was not lost on me. It was not a phenomenon I advertised. God was, for a while, to give me a more conventional means of acquiring knowledge. Through books He would introduce me to others who had questioned and found answers. I realized that I was not going to be struck dead for questioning and that indeed, He was, with loving patience, guiding me toward understanding. He would provide a book which contained a new idea. I would read and absorb as much as I was able to understand at the moment and think quietly about what had been read and talk to whoever would listen until the next came along. It was a process which grew in intensity as I became excited by the unfolding knowledge. There were times when I was so anxious for the next book that I would plead with God to show me where to look. I have had books literally fall off the shelf at my feet. Once I was standing in a book store studying the book titles when a young man walked by, pulled out a book and handing it to me said, "try this one."

Some people are awed by supernatural or unusual occurrences. I learned to expect them. I accepted God on His own terms, believing that for Him nothing was impossible and learned that life was pregnant with possibilities. He (God) encouraged me toward the exploration of truths I had not conceived of. Truths which shed light on the teachings of the Christ and made them so simple I could not see why man and his theology had found them so difficult to understand.

To those who would question these truths, their source, my means of acquiring them or their validity, I can only answer that my petition was to God. His response was one of loving guidance given in direct proportion to my ability to understand at a particular stage in my development. "Is there a man among you who, if his son asked for bread, would give him a stone?" (Luke 11:11). The guidance evolved as the truths were absorbed and understood. I was never rushed, never pushed forward until I was ready. There were times when I chafed at being denied knowledge I was not ready to understand. I remember praying very deeply some years ago for an answer. I do not recall the question but I remember quite vividly the reply. I was told in a distinctly male voice, "You must be patient you are not yet ready for the truth." I understand the wisdom of this statement now, at the time I just wanted to know everything. I did not realize that it is necessary for one to prepare for certain kinds of knowledge.

The desperation of the moment was eased by *The Power of Positive Thinking* by Dr. Norman Vincent Peale. I learned how to live one moment, one day at a time and how to use each moment as a stepping stone to guide myself up and out of the despair and into the light. The pain does not go away. The object is not to make the pain go away. The lesson is learning to live with the pain.

I had asked God for understanding and trusted Him to provide the answers. Some took longer than others to find their way into my consciousness. Many are still floating around out there awaiting my comprehension. I took God at His word and slowly as I was able to understand the door eased open. Through that door came my third child, a son. Patrick Shane Idol was born April 29, 1964, exactly two years and seven days after his sister.

Michelle...
she was the catalyst.
she taught me to live one day at the time.
She taught me to trust God to provide understanding
when I was able to accept it.

CHAPTER II

THE TOUCH OF THE MASTER'S HAND

It seems that all the events of my life have been preparation for something. I have read accounts of others and their discovery of spiritual truths. Many were very dramatic and often came as sudden revelations or encounters with extraordinary beings who opened their eyes to the truth or imparted profound wisdom. There were those who were born gifted and had from birth possessed exceptional psychic gifts. My experience was none of these. It was slow, plodding, and at times quite painful. A step by grueling step journey down a path that, once begun, must be continued. The path became my teacher. It was rarely straight and level, but paved with a mixture of obstacles, and full of twists and turns. Each experience, each encounter, each tiny ripple in the path carried within it its own lesson. Learning to view each incident of my life as a learning experience was a lesson in itself. I can look back and see that some of the knowledge came from the most unexpected sources. All taught me not to rely solely on my five senses, but to look for the unexpected possibilities even where there seemed to be the least likelihood of them occurring.

One of the major turning points on the path occurred in 1981 when I was forced to undergo a Renal Angioplasty. For those of you who do not know, an Angioplasty is a surgical procedure in which a catheter containing a small balloon is inserted through a large hollow needle into, in my case, the femoral artery in the groin and directed, by means of an x-ray viewing screen, into the renal (kidney) artery where the balloon is inflated to open an obstructed artery. Today the procedure is a fairly common one, in 1981 it was not. It had only been used for two years and mostly on cardiac patients. The arteries of the heart are relatively straight, making the procedure easier since the catheter is a floppy tube guided by a thin wire. The renal arteries are curved and more difficult to traverse.

At the age of thirty-four I developed high blood pressure. I had, in fact, had brief episodes for my entire adult life but it had always subsided of its own accord. This time, however, it was decided I would need medication. This seemed to be of no consequence, my whole family suffered from either high blood pressure or heart disease and all had been treated successfully with medication. After four years of controlling my pressure it began to climb again. There was no cause for alarm the doctor assured me, I had simply become immune to the present medication and all that was needed was a change. The only difficulty being the vast number of medications available and finding just the right one for me. Thus began two vexing years of changing medications, sometimes every two weeks, experimenting with dosages and combinations in a desperate attempt to control a steadily rising, increasingly volatile blood pressure. At one point I was taking ten pills a day including a combination of medicine to lower the pressure and diuretics to drain excess fluid from my body. I also was forced to take very large amounts of potassium supplements, because my body was rapidly being drained of its supply and the levels were critically low. Still the pressure would not drop below 150 over 110 and rose dangerously at the slightest provocation. I was rapidly becoming a "zombie" due to the ever increasing levels of medication. I would forget in the middle of a sentence what I was saying. I often fell asleep sitting up and was growing weaker every day from the loss of potassium. In short, I was a walking stroke looking for a place to happen. My doctor was understandably frustrated. He had consulted cardiologists to no avail. Kidney x-rays revealed nothing. Finally, one of the medicines seemed to take hold, I had taken it for three weeks with good results. The doctor was relieved and agreed to allow me to have a small lump removed from my arm. I checked into the hospital as an outpatient. The nurse was doing my preliminary work up, taking my blood pressure with a computerized machine. The machine began beeping, with warning lights going off. The nurse kicked the machine, complaining of malfunction and remarked that she would have to call a maintenance man to fix it. She took my pressure again just to be sure. The result was the same. I asked what seemed to be wrong and she replied that the machine was reading my pressure at 230 over 120 and that had to be a mistake. Calmly, I informed her that it was most likely correct. She turned ashen as she asked about my history, my medicine, and if I had taken it that morning. She rather frantically cautioned me not to move and hurried from the room to get her supervisor.

I was back at the doctor's office again. He confessed that he had exhausted all his ideas for treatment and confided that while all the tests had proven negative, his gut instincts told him there was a physical cause. He had made an appointment for me to see a kidney specialist. Thank God for his persistence and his gut instincts. The specialist performed all the tests available, all came back negative. There was only one test left to try. It is called a Standing Rennin. It is a very complicated blood test designed to detect the presence of an enzyme called Rennin. If this enzyme is present in excessive amounts it is indicative of an obstruction in the renal artery and usually indicates severe kidney damage. At the end of two weeks I received a call from the doctor asking that I come by his office so that we might discuss the test results. I sat looking at the grave expression on his face as he explained that to be significant the level of rennin in the blood must be at least 1.9. The level of rennin in my blood was 5.8. He had scheduled an arteriogram in three days time to pinpoint the exact location of any blockage and to determine the seriousness of the damage to my kidneys.

I was terrified of having the arteriogram. I had enough experience in medicine to understand how dangerous the procedure was for someone in my condition. In addition to the instability of my blood pressure was the fact that I was allergic to the dye that must be injected for the x-rays. It was necessary to prepare me with steroids for at least twenty four hours beforehand. To add to my already mounting apprehension, everyone insisted on telling me the experiences and horror stories of their relatives who had undergone similar procedures. In the elevator going down to the x-ray department an employee engaged me in conversation, asking what I was going down for. When I replied she asked gently if I were frightened. I burst into tears. A friend, whom I had known for years, was an x-ray technician. Seeing my name on the schedule, she asked to be assigned to my case.

When I came in she made every effort to reassure me and promised that she would be there with me through the entire procedure. The arteriogram proved to be more anxiety provoking than painful and at long last provided enough information to diagnose my illness and to recommend a course of treatment. I have a very rare, genetic kidney disease called Renal Arterial Fibro Muscular Hyper Plasia. What that long tongue twister means is that the muscle tissue surrounding my renal arteries is fibroid or malformed and squeezes off the arteries in varying degrees, seriously restricting the blood flow to my kidneys.

The left kidney was affected but not as seriously as the right. The right artery was 95% closed and the right kidney had atrophied to half the normal size. I was rapidly becoming a celebrity in local medical circles. I had an hereditary disorder that affected only 5% of the world population. None of the doctors treating me had ever seen a case before and were anticipating the challenge of devising effective treatment. I was called in after the x-rays had been studied and decisions on a course of action made. There were two options, artery bypass surgery which would entail at least three weeks in bed, or there was a relatively new and promising procedure called an Angioplasty with a much shorter recovery period and a much lower financial cost. The doctors were recommending the latter. If it failed they would perform a bypass. I sensed something tentative in his manner and asked for "the bottom line."

"Well," he began, looking at his hands which lay clasped together in his lap, "Your's is a trial run and an accurate prognosis is difficult. We don't know if the catheter will go through the artery, it may be too constricted. If the catheter goes through, we can't be certain that when the balloon is inflated it will not rupture the artery. The kidney has never had adequate blood supply. We can not be certain that if we open the artery and the blood comes rushing in, the kidney will not rupture. We will try to prepare for every consequence. We will have an operating room standing by and a supply of blood on hand just in case."

Boy, talk about being sorry you asked! Even I knew that in a worst case scenario there was little chance that they could get me to an operating room before I bled to death. The doctor wanted to schedule the procedure in three days. I refused. It was two weeks before Christmas and if things went sour I did not want that memory to forever mar Christmas for my family. I told him that I had some thinking to do and would call him after Christmas. He was apprehensive and cautioned me that without treatment my chances were slim to none, at least with treatment I had a chance. I promised I would be back in January.

I had always been a fighter, but in order to fight I must know the enemy. I had learned early that doing battle with phantoms was a precious waste of energy. Now that I knew the name of the enemy I could prepare to do battle. I kept the negative aspects of what was about to happen to myself. I can not remember being afraid. I only remember being tired. A depth of fatigue no word can adequately characterize.

I prayed for courage. I prayed for the strength to do what I must.

On January 7, I was wheeled into an x-ray room filled with interested observers from various hospitals and medical practices. I had been given a light sedative to take the edge off of my anxiety but not enough to render me unconscious. I must remain awake so that any complication or adverse reaction could be detected instantly. When I asked how long it would take, they could give me no clear cut answer.

An hour, possibly less, they speculated. The catheter was inserted and withdrawn several times in the course of two hours. Each time the hole in the artery where the needle was positioned grew dangerously larger and began to leak blood. Still the catheter could not breech the obstruction. The doctors retreated to a corner, conferring in whispers their backs to me. It was not going well. I was completely relaxed and calm. Finally, the younger of the doctors and the primary radiologist on my case came to the table to speak with me.

Laying a comforting hand on my arm he began, "We have not been able to pass the catheter through the affected area. I know you have been here a long time and are uncomfortable, but I would like to try once more. However, if you say stop we will stop. The decision is yours."

There was something in his manner that assured me that he was not doing this for his own notoriety but was genuinely concerned for me. "OK," I said, "I think I have enough joy juice left for one more try." I closed my eyes and asked, "Dear Father, they can not seem to make it go through. Can you?" I felt a sense of calm well being descend upon me as the procedure began once more. The quiet of the room was interrupted as a cheer and applause erupted from the twenty or so spectators. I opened one eye and looking at the doctor asked, "Does that mean we're in?"

"Oh yeah babe! We're in," he smiled. "Hang on, now comes the tricky part." He cautioned that when the balloon was inflated I would feel intense pain, but its duration would only be a moment or two. The pain that I felt did not have the predicted level of intensity. They seemed surprised. He remarked that most people screamed or cried out when the balloon was inflated. There were flow scans performed to be sure the artery was opened sufficiently and after approximately three hours I was returned to my room. It is necessary after an invasive procedure into an artery to keep the affected area motionless for at least six hours so that the hole made by the needle can close. A small x was drawn over the pulse point in the top of my foot and nurses dutifully checked the pulse every hour to be sure no obstructions occurred from blood clots. The following day for approximately eight hours my blood pressure dropped to normal for the first time in six years. After that time it gradually began to creep up again because of the damage still present in the left artery, but the worst of the damage had been repaired. Instead of taking ten pills a day I now only needed one. The potassium levels, however, stubbornly refused to return to normal regardless of how much supplement was given. After about six months I had a dream in which I was eating red grapes. The dream was so vivid I awoke with the taste of grapes in my mouth. The next day I bought red grapes and began eating a large bunch every day. At the end of the week when my potassium was checked the levels had "spontaneously" returned to normal. That is how the doctor explained it. He was skeptical about the "grape dream" theory. I was not skeptical about any of what I considered to be divine intervention. There was no prognosis given about how long the artery would remain open. It was hoped that with the proper blood flow the kidney would return to normal size, but there were no other cases to compare mine to. We could only wait and see. So far it is eleven years and still holding, the size of the kidney has increased, and anytime the potassium levels drop I begin eating red grapes and they return to normal.

As miraculous as this story is medically, an even more miraculous change took place spiritually. The change defies words and was not some blinding revelation or booming voice issuing from a bolt of lightening and a clap of thunder. The quiet sense of well being which descended upon me while I lay on that x-ray table has persisted. In that moment of trust, when the Father touched me with His divine hand, a connection was made that would forever change my perception of life. I no longer felt apprehensive about recovery or about anything really. Somewhere within I knew that all would be accomplished in its own time. For the first time in my life I became visionary, if only temporarily. The phenomenon faded after about two months and I was not sad to see it go. The change in my outlook remained, however, and was so complete that it was apparently reflected externally. Many of my friends, even my husband Charlie, remarked that I looked different somehow. Where I had once been a high strung, competitive worrier, I was now convinced that God's holy plan was unfolding in the universe and the wisdom of it could be completely trusted. There was absolutely no cause for fear.

> *Pain is the crucible*
> *of creativity,*
> *etching on the soul*
> *intricate patterns*
> *of divine thought.*
> (8/85)

CHAPTER III

SHANE

Shane is the Irish Gallic form of John, meaning the gift of God. When he was born his Dad said that any boy who looked that much like his Mother should be named for her. So, he was given the masculine form of my name, Patrick. From his first breath he marched to a different drummer. It's funny, everyone who knew him saw him differently. The boy I knew was mischievous, funny, sometimes careless, very affectionate and not at all what he seemed to be on the surface. He seemingly had no shining gifts that you noticed right away other than a stunningly handsome face. To know Shane required a great deal of deep study and an extraordinary amount of patience. Unwilling to be too closely scrutinized, he allowed others to assume whatever they chose about him without explanation.

He was a hyperactive child. You could not keep him still and his curiosity was insatiable. He was not intentionally destructive, he just wanted to know how things were put together and how they worked. He had an annoying habit of dismantling everything with moving parts until his curiosity was satisfied, then he wanted you to put it back together again so it would work properly. He never mastered the "putting back together" part. At the age of six months, after diagnosing his hyperactivity, the doctor warned me not to let him out of my sight. Easy for him to say. You blinked your eyes and he was gone. By his second birthday I was becoming frayed around the edges. He was impossible to get to sleep and rarely slept through the night. It was commonplace to go into the kitchen each morning and find him contentedly seated atop the refrigerator browsing through the cabinets. He ate because he had to in order to survive. As a child he cared little for food. He disputed every rule of good health. Yet he never had a cavity in his teeth, was sick less than his brother and sister, and when grown to manhood was 6 ft. 1 in.

29

tall and weighed 190 lbs. He was, by turns, the most frustrating and the most unselfishly loving person I've ever known. I used to laugh and say he was the only three year old eccentric I had ever known. Just when I thought I would strangle him he would crawl into my lap give me a big hug and say, "I love you mama."

He tore through life, recklessly it seemed to me. It was as if he had to experience everything and knew he had very little time to do so. I was never afraid for my other children the way I was afraid for him. He seemed to be afraid of nothing. I would often find him perched on the roof with an umbrella playing para-trooper. I gave up watching him play by the time he was six. He was making me old before my time.

He took baths under duress. Baths were not for washing they were for staging sea battles with toy boats. It was usually neces-sary to mop the bathroom from floor to ceiling after these battles. He was the only kid I've ever seen who could spend an hour in the tub and still look dirty.

From a very early age he was fascinated by anything to do with the Revolutionary War. When he was about 3 or 4 years old there was a TV show he liked to watch on the subject. One night as we were watching he turned to me and said, "Mother, [he never called me mother] you do understand what revolution is don't you?"

He proceeded to give me such a detailed sophisticated expla-nation that I was left speechless. It was not a child speaking to me at that moment, but a very complex intelligent person. His personality was filled with contradictions. He spoke constantly of his grandfather. He told stories of going sailing and how his grandfather often took him when he sailed his boat. I didn't think much of it at the time, small children often spin yarns and have vivid imaginations. One day when he was telling me the latest episode in the adventures of he and his grandfather I decided to play along. I said, "What's your grandfather's name?" He replied very matter-of-factly, "Grandfather."

OK… I asked about the boat, "Oh, your grandfather is a sailor on a boat?"

"No mama," he replied. "He's the captain. It's his boat."

I was becoming intrigued.

"Is it a sail boat like daddy likes," I said trying a new tack.

"Un-uh, it's like that one," he said, jumping up onto the couch to point out a picture of a square rigger ship, circa 1700's, hanging on the den wall. He didn't generalize by including all the ship pictures in the group. He pointed to a specific ship. It seemed to be the type of ship he was indicating. I didn't quite know what to say. The stories were a little beyond the usual childhood yarns, but he was unshakable, so I just kind of let it drop for a while. He did not tell the stories often after that and finally they stopped altogether. While I was still interested by the strange seemingly factual stories coming from such a small boy, he simply refused to be pressed for details. He did not like explaining his deeper thoughts when he was not sure others would understand. He would simply say, "Oh, I just made it up," or, "I was just kidding."

I became very familiar with that dodge over the years. It was a line he used when pressed for information he did not wish to give or could not explain. The stories stopped and I thought no more of it until a year or so later. He was about five years old. I was in the kitchen when he came in and crawled up on the kitchen counter and sat, watching me work. You could always tell when he had something on his mind. He would become your shadow, sitting beside you, following you around, shuffling back and forth sometimes for an hour or two, trying to muster the courage to ask you the big question. There was no use pressing him, he would not ask until he had it straight in his own mind exactly what he wanted to say. Finally he blurted out, "Mama, do you believe in reincarnation?" I was dumbfounded. I had no idea a child his age even knew what the word meant. "Yes, I think I do," I stammered, "Why do you ask?"

"I just wondered ," he said, "I think I do, too."

With that he jumped down off the counter and went out to play. That was Shane, simple and to the point. He rarely wasted words. I don't think he often shared this thoughtful, mystical side of his nature with anyone except me. Perhaps because he knew of my intense study and need to understand the deeper aspects of being.

Encountering this aspect of his nature always seemed to startle people, perhaps because they were so distracted by his behavior and rarely looked beyond it. No one knew this better than he and he could use their lack of awareness to disarm on occasion.

When he entered the first grade he was given the same teacher who had taught his older brother Chris. I had cautioned her at the outset not to compare the boys. They were as different as their coloring. Shane had dark curly hair and amber eyes, Chris reddish blonde hair and blue eyes. Chris was a model student, an extremely intelligent, well behaved perfectionist who did anything anyone else could do better. Shane, on the other hand, was wiggly, couldn't concentrate and was more interested in playing in the creek than in learning his ABC's. His teacher had called, requesting a conference. She was understandably frustrated and had become more so by an incident that had happened that day. Her opening question took me off guard. She asked, rather tentatively, if one of our children had died. Taken aback I replied that we had lost a daughter. She expressed her sympathy and asked how recently it had happened. I told her that the baby had died two years before Shane was born. She was silent for a moment then asked, "have you been discussing it at home recently?"

I explained that while we did not avoid the subject we had not been discussing it within recent memory.

"Why do you ask?"

"Well," she began hesitantly, "this morning I looked up and Shane was standing beside my desk staring at me. I asked him what was wrong and he said, 'My sister died.' "

I could tell by her voice that the incident had shaken her deeply.

"He seemed so forlorn, his grief so profound, I just assumed that it had happened recently. She died two years before he was born?" she puzzled. "Do you have any idea why it would be on his mind?" she said, completely overwhelmed by his sensitivity.

"No," I replied, "none," feeling a warm unpleasant little tingling crawl up an imaginary cord through the center of my being. It was a feeling I would come to associate with foreboding and warning. I did not press him about it, nor did the teacher. I had become aware of some inexplicable bond between my two middle children. It was nothing I could put my finger on and I didn't approach Shane with my suspicions. It would take him fourteen years, until the age of twenty, before he would finally explain.

School was a big chore for both of us. He hated it and I was weary of trying to come up with new incentives. I had tried everything from begging and pleading to threats. Nothing seemed to work. Little boys are restless enough, but when you add hyperactivity and its short attention span you have a teachers nightmare. The concept of hyperactive children was still fairly new at that time and for the most part these children were considered problem children or just plain bad kids. Complicating an already impossible situation even further, was the fact that he was a first generation "busing" child. By the time he was in the sixth grade he had been in a different school each year. I would go in twice every year for conferences. The teachers would shake their head in frustration and say, "What can I tell you... He is a sweet little boy and so beautiful. He has a very bright mind. I just don't know how to get to it." I tried helping him with his studies at home, but we would both become frustrated and invariably end up in angry shouting matches. He would insist that he knew the material. I would explain that if this were so, then he had to let the teacher know that he knew it. His reply was always the same. "Why? I thought the important thing was that I knew it." It was difficult facing the teachers and their pleas for me to do something and he was only in the third grade. Most of the time we had to be content with small victories. I had flatly refused to consider the use of drugs. Finally, I decided to try the direct approach. It was time we talked about his hyperactivity to see if perhaps we could find a way to solve some of the problems. He sat crossed legged on his bed, staring intently into my eyes while I explained to him that he was different (referring to his hyperactivity) and he might have to learn to do things to help himself. I asked if there was something which calmed him, if so perhaps we could take advantage of it when he was feeling hyper. He listened without interrupting until I finished, then said in a rather grown up tone, "You know, mom, I've always known that I was different from everyone else, I just didn't know why."

I had the eeriest sensation that he was talking about something else, though I was not sure what. He said almost as an afterthought that drawing and music calmed him. He was like that sometimes. I would be talking to him and get the distinct impression that he was talking about something entirely different. A couple of times I asked him about it and he would smile that closed mouthed "Stan Laurel" grin of his and say, "Just playing head games with you ma." He played "head games" a lot, particularly with me. He used to tease me and tell me I was so gullible he couldn't resist. I wonder... He never came at you straight on. It was always sideways so you wouldn't know what he was up to.

"Head games" aside, he did show steady improvement as he neared puberty and in some subjects showed real accomplishment. They seemed to be the subjects that were taught by lecturing such as history, biology, and his favorite, psychology. He often gave the impression that he was daydreaming and not paying attention. He would stare out a window or off into the distance with that far away look in his eye. If you scolded him, without flicking an eyelash nor changing the direction of his gaze, he would say, "I'm listening." One frustrated teacher in a fit of temper called him on it and asked him to repeat what she had said. He turned to her calmly and repeated verbatim every word she had uttered since entering the room. "Head games."

He was a puzzle to his teachers. He had a very high IQ, yet most of the time was an under achiever. He would answer questions in class, often trick questions that no one else could answer, yet he would not, or could not, answer the same questions on paper for a test. I personally thought he had some sort of perception problem or learning disability. He had a great deal of difficulty expressing himself on paper and his spelling was atrocious. Once when he was about eight years old a vacant house in our neighborhood was vandalized. Windows were broken, and profane words were spray painted on the back of the house. For a time all of the children in the neighborhood were suspect. One night Charlie and I were discussing it and he jokingly asked if all the words were spelled correctly. When I replied that they were, he quipped, "Then Shane didn't write any of them. He would have spelled it *shirt*."

I always felt he had a very intelligent mind looking for a way to adequately express itself. The perpetual motion aspect of his hyperactivity seemed to subside in his teens. The short attention span and his eccentricities persisted, however, and became a part of his charm. He came to eating, bathing, and sleeping late and had some time to make up for. He took marathon showers. The family was convinced that he slept in the shower they were so long. The downstairs ceiling was in a constant state of repair because water continually seeped from the shower above. When he needed to catch up on his sleep he would shower before going to bed and sleep fully clothed complete with shoes, and baseball cap, just so he could sleep an extra 20 minutes in the morning. We used to laugh and say he was like an old "tom cat." He would burn the candle at both ends for two or three days, hardly sleeping. Then, when on the verge of collapse, he would crawl upstairs wrap up in his "special" quilt and sleep in front of the TV until hunger forced him awake which could be as much as twenty four hours later. Chris teased him, telling him he looked as if he had been shot and flung out of a speeding car.

By the age of eighteen he was a walking garbage disposal. If it didn't move he ate it. When dinner was on the table he would joke, "This is fine for me what is everyone else going to eat?" In high school he held the record for the number of sausage biscuits consumed by one human being and was quite proud of the fact that he could belch the national anthem. He was a funny kid. He had a rather slap stick sense of humor and seemed to enjoy the notoriety that surrounded his escapades. Family gatherings invariably came around to laughing and telling, "Shane stories." They seemed to be endless.

He always said he went to school to get out and showed no inclination toward continuing his education beyond high school. He was more interested in being in the military. After high school graduation he tried to enlist in the Navy but could not pass the physical. Each time he was examined his blood pressure was elevated and even though he agreed to sign a waiver they refused to accept him. He was bitterly disappointed. Odd how fate steps in sometimes. It was a few months later that he began talking of going to college. A year after graduating from high school he entered a local community college to study electronics. The first few months were difficult but the school was a small one and he got a lot of one on one attention and the cogs slowly began to slip into place. His writing became more sophisticated and he gained confidence in himself. He seemed to have found his niche. He earned an associates degree in electronics and decided to continue his studies toward an engineering degree. This from a kid who had taken remedial math in high school. I think that mind had pushed the door open and was coming out. He was in many respects a paradox. If you looked at the surface and did not delve beneath you missed the real essence of Shane. It was a game with him. He would not tell you how he felt and what he thought. He wanted you to be interested enough to find out for yourself.

He had a weakness for the mavericks and the displaced of this world and they seemed to trail him around like puppies. He had a patient understanding of human failings and weaknesses in others and a desire to make a difference by helping those who had difficulty helping themselves. He had absorbed so much negative input himself, trying to figure out how he, as a square peg, could fit into a round hole. Rather than making him bitter and resentful, however, it made him patient and understanding. He worked for several years in a sheltered work shop, helping with handicapped workers and often assisted with Special Olympics. I always admired his ability to treat the handicapped with dignity and no trace of awkwardness. He spoke of them gently and lovingly. He loved to tease and joke with them, refusing to recognize their handicap as a barrier to fun. He always laughed with them, never at them. There was one particular girl he spoke of often. She was seventeen or eighteen. I am not sure what her handicap was, but she had never grown to normal height and walked only with the aid of crutches. Shane was fond of teasing her by stacking the cartons she needed out of her reach. When she complained he told her he had come up with a new kind of therapy called climbing for cartons. Her reply was a resounding whack across his shins with her crutch. The teasing always ended with the two of them chasing each other giggling and laughing as she tried to trip him up. Another time when he had been his usual teasing self all through his shift, in retaliation the workers as they were leaving took toilet paper and "rolled" his truck. Both he and they seemed to delight in their teasing and pranks. They shared a mutual fondness for one another.

He never missed the opportunity to encourage someone who needed a boost. The odd thing about his methods was that people rarely knew they were being helped. He would simply blend in with the group he happened to be with and help however he felt he could without drawing too much attention to himself. His gift was a subtle one. He had the ability to give others strength and courage and make them feel good about themselves. When he was present everyone had fun and there was always laughter, often at his expense, but he didn't seem to mind. He never seemed to take himself too seriously and that quality was contagious. He would tease me when I scolded him by singing the David Allen Coe song, "I'm just an old chunk of coal, but I'm gonna be a diamond some day."

I don't mean to paint him with too fine a brush. He was a rascal and it was by turns his most endearing and most irritating quality. Some thought that is all that he was, but I knew differently. He would let me see inside occasionally. He told me things, which I did not understand at the time, but he knew how my mind worked and that I would remember and understand one day. One of the most memorable times was when he had just turned twenty. We were having one of our late night discussions which often went into the wee hours of the morning. It was a custom I enjoyed with each of my children as they matured. The subjects varied and were often no deeper than school gossip, their hopes and dreams, or their latest relationship with the opposite sex. Occasionally though, the discussions delved into philosophies and allowed each of us the opportunity of letting down the barriers and instead of being parent and child to simply be two people sharing our deepest feelings with one another. This was one of those times. I can no longer remember what prompted the discussion but the subject was death. He was saying that he didn't think he had understood death until the age of eight when his great grandfather had died. He had asked to view the body. I, afraid of the affect it might have on so young a child, had misgivings. His dad felt he should be allowed to if he wished. Chris and I did not care to go in so, Shane and his dad went alone. He had never spoken of it or his feelings about it until this night. He was explaining that like most small children he had not understood the finality of death. We discussed children's reactions to death, our own personal feelings on funerals, and the hereafter. The subject, as always, came around to Michelle. I was trying to explain how devastated I had been by her death and how it had been the catalyst which had sent me in search of answers about life after death. He said, "I talk to Michelle, mom." He just kind of blurted it out, not certain of my reaction, but feeling the time had come for me to know. "I've seen and talked to her," he repeated. I stared at him and time seemed suspended. There was a look in his eyes that I had never seen before, a completely unguarded view of his soul look. A look that dispelled any lack of credibility about what he was telling me. His secret was out. Still he did not elaborate. He offered nothing but that one disclosure and awaited my reaction before going on. He had never learned the art of subterfuge. If he did not want you to know something he would not discuss it. If you asked a direct question he would answer honestly, but you must ask exactly what you wanted to know. He volunteered nothing. He answered each of my questions in turn never going beyond the boundaries of that particular answer. I asked him to describe her. His faced softened as he said, "She's beautiful. She has long dark hair and blue eyes." I still was not completely convinced that this was not just a ruse to comfort me. I asked how he knew it was her. He replied that he was not certain how he knew, he just did. I asked all the questions I could think of and he patiently and quietly answered each one. They met somewhere beyond the ordinary level of consciousness in a place he described as a green meadow with beautiful grass and trees. Where this reality existed he could not say, only that it did. They sat on a hill in the grass under a tree and talked. She was always the age he was at the time and was always there when things were most difficult for him, to warn him when he was reckless, or to encourage him when he was down. She had been his constant companion since birth and because of her loving presence he explained that he did not understand what it meant to be lonely. My suspicions about a bond between them were confirmed. Somewhere within my being a door swung open and a beautiful radiant light streamed through. He would later take my hand and with a love that transcended this world show me what lay beyond that door. We never spoke of it again.

He seemed quiet and retiring as he entered his twenties. He was very soft spoken and though not shy, preferred to blend in with others rather than stand out. While he had a nice, well-developed body he seemed never to fully command it no matter how hard he worked at perfecting a physical skill. In the end his body balked at agility and clumsily failed him. It was as if being in a physical body was foreign to him. What he lacked in agility he more than made up for in sheer brute toughness. He loved football. It was the one sport he could hold his own in simply because he could take an ungodly pounding and never complain. One of his coaches once remarked that Shane was by no means the most talented athlete he had coached but he was by far the toughest. He never backed down, he never whined, and he never quit. Shane rarely complained of anything really, pain, mistreatment, or injustice. When he did we usually took notice because it was a sign that he had been pushed to his absolute limit. His tolerance of pain, whether physical or mental was extraordinary. He was in a word, controlled, so much so that some mistakenly believed he did not care about anything. Evidence to the contrary was the fact that his nails were continually bitten off to the quick and for most of his life he had chronic digestive problems. One testimony to his capacity to endure pain came on a May evening of his twenty-first year. He was finishing up the last days of his two year stint at community college before transferring to UNC Charlotte to continue his studies in electronic engineering. He had just finished his exams. I had taken Jennifer, his younger sister, to her dance classes and returned home to find his car in the drive way. By this time he was only living at home during college breaks. Jennifer was excited. The two had been practically joined at the hip since her birth when he was eight and one half years old. She bounded up the stairs, anticipating his usual "bear hug" greeting. Her alarm at what she saw was reflected in her tone of voice as she called me to come quickly. He was lying on his bed pale, sweaty and complaining of a stomach ache, dizziness, and fever. The little trickle of dread that inched up the center of my being warned me that this was not a stomach virus or something he had eaten. We met the doctor at the emergency room, and a surgeon was called. It was decided that he would undergo an appendectomy, not because his symptoms were classic, but because in an otherwise healthy twenty-one year old they could think of no other cause for his illness. I tried to tell them nothing about that boy's life had ever been classic. To make a long story short, after five anxious AM hours the doctor came out to speak with me. The exhaustion etched in his face and the care with which he selected his words spoke volumes. Not only did Shane have appendicitis but his appendix had been ruptured for at least two weeks. The appendix was out of place and tucked up behind the small intestine causing a baseball size abscess to form on the outside wall of the intestine. The intestine had been about to perforate and his entire abdominal cavity was filled with acute peritonitis (infection of the abdominal cavity lining). I think the doctor's exact words were, "He couldn't have more damage if he had swallowed a live hand grenade." Needless to say, things would be touch and go and extremely critical for some time. The doctors assured me that he must have been in absolute agony for days, yet Shane only admitted to having pain for a couple of days. He later confessed he had been in pain for several weeks but he didn't want to worry me. He never wanted to worry me. I could never convince him that some of the things he did to prevent me from worrying often caused me to worry more. I am convinced that the sheer power of our prayers kept him here. He said he had dreamed about his surgery weeks before. He dreamed of many things and hinted at the prophetic nature of their contents, but when pressed for details always seemed to avoid the subject.

All my children were aware of my fascination with spiritual development. One of the aspects I had studied a great deal was dreams. I had found them to be a helpful way of exploring myself and had for years kept a dream journal. The children often related dreams of their own, asking me to try and interpret them. Shane came home for the weekend and in the course of conversation mentioned that he was having a recurring dream and asked what I thought. In the dream he was a young military officer stationed aboard a ship. He was in his quarters seated on his bunk. Each dream was the same setting but expanded on the theme each time. The next dream he was told that there was going to be an inspection and he was trying to get his quarters cleaned and in order. The next, one of his fellow officers ran in and warned that the captain was coming. The next, he could hear the captains footsteps in the hall. He asked if I thought it meant he would be a naval officer after college. He stared at me intently, waiting for my answer. I quipped, "Well it's possible. What do you think it means?" His reply was lost as others entered the room and joined the conversation.

I was beginning to notice a subtle change in Shane. He was often silent. I would look up and find him staring at me. He would quickly look away. I tried not to dwell on it too much, after all he had been through a very critical illness. He was going to a larger college, a lot of adjustments. He often asked hypothetical questions for "friends" at school which I answered as best I could. They were usually questions about religion and related subjects and frequently sounded rather odd somehow. He went through the motions, but something had changed. He came home each week-end, requesting that we pick him up. It was a ninety minute drive one way and I suggested he take his truck back to school so he could drive himself. He refused, making some excuse about parking fees.

He was home for Christmas break. He had something to tell us. I recognized the pattern. He had followed me around all night, making jokes, sliding across the wood floors like a ten year old. I waited, he said nothing. Finally his dad and I went to bed around one A.M. I had just turned out the light. He came in and sat down on the edge of the bed and flicked on the light. "I have to tell you something," he said. We sat up in bed, thinking oh boy, here it comes and it's a big one. "I'm getting married," he began, "you are going to be grandparents." He and Janet had been seeing each other for four years. They had been high school sweethearts. We knew they were in love and would marry when he finished college. We talked for a while, mainly about his plans, was he going to finish his education, how was he going to support a family? I had an unusual reaction. I was cold. I don't mean my skin was cold. My blood was pulsing through my veins, but it was ice cold and I was shivering uncontrollably. I understand now the adage about feeling your blood run cold. Shane was thanking us for always loving him, for our constant support and encouragement. He was crying. I had not seen him cry since he was five years old. He told us how much he loved us and leaned over to hug us, then stood quickly and left the room. I had heard what he said, but again I had the persistent notion that he was talking about something else.

Christmas that year was the most wonderful and laugh filled I can ever remember. The Chris and Shane comedy routine kept us all laughing constantly. The object of most of the fun seemed to center around a green velvet cake I had made for Christmas dinner. The cake is usually red velvet but there was no red cake coloring to be found that year, so I had improvised and made the cake green. The jokes flowed freely about the hazards of eating green cake.

Shane and Janet were married on December 28, in a small candle lit ceremony with mostly immediate family present. Shane's grandmother cried audibly throughout the ceremony. My mother rarely cried and could not explain why she had done so on this occasion. Shane returned to school for the second semester. I insisted he take his truck with him. He was reluctant, but he would be job hunting and needed transportation. He still came by every weekend but conversation had become stilted. He had difficulty looking me in the eye and where he had always been an affectionate teddy bear, he now avoided physical contact. I fancied, on occasion, I saw tears in his eyes. He was deeply troubled about something and I had no idea what.

January stretched out abysmally. It was always a bit of a let down after the fun of Christmas, so to relieve the hum drum Charlie and I began planning a trip to Atlantic City. The trip was planned for February. We had tickets to see Julio Iglesias at Resorts International on February 22. I was a big fan and excited by the prospect of seeing him live. Shane and Janet had agreed to come and spend the weekend with Jennifer while we made the trip. The week of our trip came and my excitement was building. It was Tuesday morning February 19, I was up at 6 AM to get Jennifer off to school. My sleep had been disturbed the night before by that prickly feeling crawling up that imaginary cord in my being. It had awakened me at 2 AM with a feeling as if something were flying from my being as I tried to hold it back. It was not a pleasant sensation, but I refused to have my enthusiasm dampened. There was a knock at the door. I could not imagine who it could be at this hour of the morning. I opened the door to find a Sheriff's deputy standing on the porch, asking to speak with my husband. I told the deputy that my husband was sleeping and I did not want to disturb him. Charlie worked at night, getting home after 3 AM. He often got calls from work about employees who were in trouble and needed help. I had begun trying to screen out these intrusions so as not to disturb his sleep. The officer suggested I wake him. I allowed the deputy into the foyer and went to wake Charlie. The announcement was so formal. He asked if we had a son named Patrick Shane Idol. I was thinking to myself if that boy has gone and gotten himself into trouble I'm going to strangle him. At a distance I heard the deputy say, "My sad duty...your son Patrick...fatally injured... car accident." "Fatally," I kept thinking, "what does fatally mean? Oh, God, Oh, God, fatally means dead." Something inside me ripped open and let out a silent primal wail of agony. It's odd, you function automatically, mechanically as if from some distant detached vantage point and the strangest pictures play in your head. I kept remembering one of the first summers we lived in our house. The area was rural and many of the surrounding areas still kept farm animals. It was warm and I had the windows open. I kept hearing this cow, bawling constantly day and night. A sound so mournful and sad it haunted me. The cow belonged to one of Shane's friends and when he came home I asked if he knew what was wrong with that poor cow. He replied that she had given birth to a calf several days before and the calf had died. She was inconsolable. I understood that mother mourning for her child, her grief no more primitive than my own. There were no tears, just this unspeakably, agonizingly silent cry within, too painful to emit.

> Shane...
> *He taught me patience.*
> *He taught me to love and*
> *accept others as they are.*
> *He taught me to be grateful for small victories.*
> *Most of all, he taught me that there*
> *is no death, only transition.*

CHAPTER IV

THE RAINBOW

When the boys were in their teens and experiencing their first encounters with romance on the shoe string budget of minimum wage, they came to me and asked what kind of gift they could give their sweetheart with so little money. I told them to go and buy a single red rose. They argued that buying only one would make them look cheap. "Oh, no," I said, "a single red rose means I love you." They, not understanding the feminine mystique countered, "But what if she doesn't know what it means?" I assured them that every female from birth knew and was enchanted by the loving symbol of a rose. A single red rose became a symbol of love and a way to charm girls for Shane. So, the afternoon after his death, after the arrangements had been made I went to the florist and bought five long stemmed red roses, one for each of us to lay atop the white blanket of flowers on the burgundy coffin as a tribute of love.

Love and expressions of love have always been important in our family. It is important to say I love you. After being told of Shane's death, Jennifer kept fretting over and over that she had not said goodbye and told him how much she loved him. She was fourteen and for all of her life, the "Kid" as he called her, had been the apple of his eye. When she was born he had insisted that if the new baby was a girl he was running away from home. When Charlie called to tell the boys that they did indeed have a new baby sister, true to his word Shane packed up his quilt, a peanut butter sandwich, bag of Fritos, and a Pepsi and set out. He was found a half hour later by Chris and his Granny around the corner of the house behind the fence where he had set up camp. His opinion changed after seeing her, however. From the moment he laid eyes on her it was love at first sight. He would sit by her crib just watching her. If her eyes fluttered he would pick her up, assuring me that she was awake. I finally had to tell him not to disturb her unless she cried. He would sit and hold her, crooning, "Mama, isn't she beautiful?" He became her adoring champion and protector. Each of them always asked the other's approval about important decisions. His girlfriends must pass muster with Jennifer or we never saw them again. He must approve her clothes, hair styles, and any other major decisions. If Shane did not approve it was canceled. He was never upset by her trailing him around and woe be to anyone who got in the way.

I think the single most comforting realization in the first few days and for all the days thereafter was the certain knowledge that we had all loved each other deeply and had continually expressed that love both in word and deed.

It was a family decision that the coffin be closed. None of us wanted our last memory of Shane to be his stiff waxen body lying in a silk lined casket. I stood for several long moments with my open palms resting on the lid of that shiny box, seeking through my fingertips some frail remnant of my son's lingering presence. Charlie came up behind me and gently laying his hand over mine whispered, "He's gone Mama." I knew that it was so. It was his going that had disturbed my sleep. I knew that now. Still I grasped for some stray wisp of being that might hesitate near his body.

The people came to attend his wake. They lined up politely one behind the other to pay their respects and offer their condolences. For over two hours that unbroken line of friends came, bringing with them their fond memories. They all represented different phases of his life and each group saw him differently. There were those who remembered the dirty faced little boy with the torn jeans who had fearlessly climbed into and walked through the sewers with them on their way home from school. There were the teachers, who while frustrated with the student, had admired the boy. There were the high school friends who remembered that when there was a party it was Shane who always stayed late to be sure that those who had, had too much to drink got home safely. I thought of how many times he and I had been round and round about his coming in past curfew. He often said he had to take several people home. When he had continually given me these excuses for missing curfew I had thought that was exactly what they were, excuses. Still, he continued, taking whatever punishment was levied for being late. The recipients of his caring sought out his brother and sister now, telling them how he had helped them. They related incidents that were more easily confided to their peers. A group of college friends had made the eighty mile trip so that they might share their remembrances with us. They had only known him six months but he had left fond memories. There was the young woman who had lost her father quite suddenly and had been staggered by the loss. Shane had encouraged her, had insisted that she keep a positive attitude and never settle for second best. He, being slightly older than the others, had organized study groups and helped them with their studies. Then there were stories of the Shane we knew who grew a stubble beard, wrapped his head in a checkered table cloth and attended the Halloween party, masquerading as Yasir Arafat. There was the time they had ordered pizza. Someone had made the mistake of betting him that he couldn't eat three large pizzas. There was the young man haunted by the running joke between them. It was the custom of the university to award a 4.0 to a student if one's roommate were killed or died. Shane had laughingly warned that they had best stay away from the windows because he needed a 4.0 real bad. There is so much negative press given to the youth of today. So much discussion about how uncaring and unfeeling they are. I saw none of that in these young people. They came, offering their help in whatever capacity it was needed. Six of his high school friends carried his coffin. His college friends carefully packed his belongings to spare his dad and brother that sad duty. They shared with his little sister photographs of fun times they had together. They sent letters to his dad and me, containing articles about Shane in the school newspaper. There had been a bonfire at a pep rally. A moment of silence had been offered in tribute to him. They thought he would have been pleased. They were correct. Seeing him through their eyes and knowing he had meant so much to so many different people gave each of us who loved him so, a warm sense of appreciation that they had shared their memories with us. Talking with all these friends, both his and ours, had been a tender celebration of life and love. I had functioned on sheer adrenaline for two days. I felt no anger, no bitterness, no sense of being robbed. Amidst this gentle outpouring of love inspired by Shane it was impossible to feel anything except tenderness.

The morning came to lay his body to rest. The services were planned for eleven and the family was up and preparing to go. Something within me shut down, refusing this final ritual. My body simply collapsed. I was distressed at not attending the services, feeling as if I were deserting my family when they needed me, but I had no strength left.

Charlie and I decided to take the trip to Atlantic City, not so much for entertainment, but as an opportunity to be alone and share our grief for our son. Jennifer spent the week-end with Chris and his wife Marion. They needed to share their grief for their brother. Each of us had lost someone different. Charlie and I had lost a son. Chris, Marion and Jennifer had lost a brother. Janet had lost a husband, and Shane's unborn child had lost a father. We all grieved for our loss. Charlie and I talked, and wept, and relived every single moment of his life with us. As we talked I could see the white shadowy image of Shane's face, floating before mine as if trying to comfort me. We agreed, then as now, that despite the pain and anguish suffered we felt privileged to have shared his love even if for only a short time.

The rituals for the living were all accomplished and we who loved him were left alone together unable to fill the vacancy created by his going. The first few days after a death you function automatically, doing what must be done, going about the business of slowly trying to let go of that beloved being whose soul has left you with a body no longer animated by its presence. The people were gone and we were left alone in a house full of echoes and visions of what once was and is no more. We were left to deal with the boxes of clothes; the empty chair at the table; the difficulty of making lasagna and cheese cake because they were his favorite meal; the navy blue dress hanging in the closet which could never be worn again because it will forever be a reminder of his wake; the anticipation of arriving home to see his car parked in the drive-way; his twenty second birthday; the birth of his son; the first Christmas without him. All these we must face. There is no running away. Somehow we must learn to release that part of ourselves which resided within him. I must let go of his hand just as I did when he took his first step, or his first day of school. I must find the courage to free his spirit and release him to his destiny, but how? Life would forever be divided into two time periods, before Shane's death and after. These were the thoughts which flooded my mind when I was alone. "Oh, God," I prayed, "It is so dark and I can't see the path. I feel so bewildered and alone, Please may I take your hand?" Then I remembered the rainbow. So much had happened and I had been so preoccupied that I had almost forgotten. Now God, hearing my plea gently took my hand and guided me to that memory. It had been on Sunday afternoon, January 20, exactly one month before Shane's death. It was a stormy, unseasonably warm day for January. Charlie and I, having nothing in particular to do, had decided to go for a Sunday afternoon drive. He took this as an opportunity to browse through several car lots in a small town near by. We were driving down a two lane country highway noting that there had moments before been a storm in the area. The dark clouds still hung heavily in the sky. I glanced ahead and what I saw took my breath away. Spanning the width of the road ahead, lay the most electric ribbon of color I had ever seen. The very air was filled with shimmering particles of color rising up out of the pavement like some giant handful of fairy dust. I was overwhelmed almost to the point of ecstasy. We actually passed right through the rainbow. I continued to exult about its beauty as we drove into the car lot. Charlie backed the car in so that I could see more clearly as he browsed through the cars. I could hardly believe my eyes. Events of this nature simply did not occur in January in our part of the country, yet there stretched out before me, spanning the breadth of that storm blackened sky was a full rainbow. I had never seen a complete bow before and the radiance of its beauty touched me so deeply that I found tears trickling down my cheeks. Something was speaking to me from deep within my soul. I know that rainbows are God's way of giving mankind hope, of promising him that he will endure. I also know that it is presumptuous of me to believe that this particular rainbow was meant for me alone, but something in me was compelled by its presence. As we drove down the highway toward home I felt somehow that I must keep my eyes fastened on the rainbow, feeling that as long as I looked at it, it would remain. When the highway eventually turned in the opposite direction and the landscape faded into the distance taking with it the rainbow, I was left with a feeling of reverence that I had been allowed to witness such dazzling beauty. I was filled with its ambiance for days. Now I understood why God had directed our path toward that glorious event. Shane was preparing to escape the prison of the body. God knew that he was coming home and this was His promise that Shane's soul lived and in time with His help the sun would come into our lives again.

> *Immortality*
> *My life closed twice before its close;*
> *It remains to see*
> *if immortality unveil a*
> *third event to me.*
> *So huge, so hopeless to conceive,*
> *as these that twice befell.*
> *Parting is all we know of heaven,*
> *and all we need of hell.*
> — Emily Dickinson

CHAPTER V

THE BUTTERFLY

God speaks to man in a soft still voice which comes from within. Sometimes it isn't a voice in the accepted sense, but more a feeling, a sense of being drawn to something which can not always be explained logically. It was in just this manner that I was introduced to my first book on spirituality. It was a cold rainy Saturday afternoon. Charlie and the boys were watching a basketball game on TV and I was bored so, I decided to go to a near-by shopping center and poke around for a while. I wandered into a drug store and after sampling all the perfumes and lipstick shades, I began scanning the magazine racks. Finding nothing of interest that I had not read, I moved on to the paper back book section. To this day I can not explain exactly what happened in the next few moments. I picked up a book, paid for it at the register and left the store. I do not recall looking at the title until I was in the car. I was both confused and surprised, for there on the seat beside me lay a book entitled *The Here and The Hereafter* by Ruth Montgomery. I had no idea what the book was about but I had always been an avid reader and could not help but be intrigued. The title of the book, as it turned out, was self explanatory and began a twenty-five year fascination with books that dealt with spiritual development. Their subject matter covered a wide range of topics concerning the origin and destiny of the soul. I have never been able to adequately explain my all consuming need to know, nor define exactly what it is I need to know. I have been like a blind man on a path, groping for something familiar so that I would feel more secure by knowing where I fit into the scheme of things. Knowledge became an insatiable giant in my life, forever needing to be fed by my continuous questions. The more it was fed the more it required. I had a mental picture of God, smiling indulgently at my infantile efforts at seeking the spiritual. I was trying, like a toddler, to walk on spiritual legs not yet strong enough to support me for more than a step or two, yet impatient to be running freely and exploring all the beauties which knowledge brings. I think there were times in the intervening years when Charlie despaired for my sanity, which I found odd since it was he who first introduced me to the world beyond the five senses. I regret to this day, laughing at what he said that first time and referring to it as superstitious nonsense. It took many years before he would freely discuss such things with me again. In fact, he often tried to discourage me from pursuing the subject further. I was perplexed by his attitude, particularly since he had such a strong psychic gift. I think secretly I was somewhat envious. I had never been particularly psychic. Though for as long as I could remember I had always had this strange inner feeling as if there was something just beyond memory's grasp, which if I squeezed my eyes shut tightly and thought deeply about I would remember. I often sensed a mysterious presence and felt that if I turned around quickly enough I could catch a glimpse of it before it vanished. I had experienced only a brief encounter with visions. I had from time to time through out my life experienced some mildly prophetic dreams, though nothing earth shaking. Voices spoke to me constantly within my mind, but to me this was nothing out of the ordinary and I did not realize that others did not hear the same thing. Sometimes the voices were clear and distinct, sometimes like a tape recorder speeded up so that the sound was only a twitter. At other times it was difficult to distinguish between the voices and my thoughts. I suppose the most earth shaking thing I can remember of a metaphysical nature was practicing astral projection as a child. Perhaps practicing is not the correct word, since it seemed to be purely involuntary and in no way consciously controlled by me. I was not aware of what I had done until my reading explained. It is apparently a fairly common phenomenon among children, particularly unhappy children, and I was often that.

I was now faced with putting all that I had learned and all that I believed to the test. It was Friday night, nine days after Shane's death and I was alone, really alone, for the first time since his death. A friend had called and talked at length, encouraging me and trying to lift my spirits. As they had been since his death my thoughts were filled with Shane. I was wondering if his spirit was still near and if he could hear me. I said aloud, "Sweetheart, are you here? If so is there anyway you can let me know?" On the wall to my right above the couch hung a basket containing a plant. It began to swing rhythmically. I sat transfixed, staring at the basket which swung for a full five minutes by the clock then stopped dead still. I was not sure what to think. I was not convinced that I was not somehow making the plant move. I got up and tried to swing the basket on its bracket. Though I tried repeatedly, it would swing no more than twice in succession before coming to a complete stop. I was not certain what to believe. Believing in unproven theories is one thing, but how does one resolve the reality of the existence of the soul, not in some far away place beyond our present reality, but right here and now in the room with you? This, I would find, was only the beginning of a series of events which would occur not only for me, but for each member of the family, convincing us beyond a shadow of a doubt that not only had Shane survived death, but he was close by. I was still deciding what to tell the rest of the family, not completely convinced that they would buy the swinging plant, even as hungry as we all were for some indication that Shane still lived. At breakfast the next morning Charlie related a dream he had in which he had seen a group of people wearing light colored hooded robes ascending a stair case. As he had stood watching, one had turned to look at him, nodding in acknowledgment. The face framed by the soft hood had been Shane's. I decided to tell him about the incident with the plant. He smiled softly, indicating his acceptance of the validity of Shane's presence. I cleared the breakfast dishes and went to get dressed. I was brushing my teeth when I heard Shane's gleeful voice quite distinctly say, "Boy, not having to fool with that body is great!" I was aware of the lovely spring morning outside my window, of the sound of birds singing, then suddenly there was this euphoric rushing sensation entering the top of my head. I realized from my knowledge of astral projection that a soul had either entered or departed my body. It did not feel as if my soul had departed. There was no sense of viewing the body at a distance, just this incredibly joyful euphoria and a sense that Shane was near.

Jennifer, as was her custom on Saturday morning, had taken her breakfast upstairs to the den to watch TV. I joined her later to tell her of my revelations, feeling it might offer her some comfort. As I told her she turned to look at me quickly and nodded. "I know, mama," she said, "I was sitting here watching TV and the door to his room opened and he came out, walked into the den, and sat down with me, just like he used to."

My feelings fluctuated between elation and attempts at objectivity. I could not be sure that we were not, out of our intense need, conjuring up these images to assuage our grief. I had no point of reference, no way to measure our experiences against those of others. In the next few weeks I thought deeply and often about what was happening. We as a family shared our experiences and thoughts and found strength in the sharing. We were not frightened, nor did we want the visits, whatever their explanation to end. After the first week or so the apparitions subsided. In early March I had an extremely vivid dream, which to me, explained why they had ended. I was in a large house cluttered with furniture. I was apparently going to clean up the house and restore it to some sort of order. I was checking all the rooms to decide which furniture to keep and which to discard. I went to the second floor of the house opened a door and there on a bed, covered in a blue blanket, lay Shane sleeping. I had read that after the soul departs the body it is often necessary for them to "sleep" for a period of time in order to make the transition from the physical plane to the spiritual less traumatic. I was comforted to know that he was sleeping and sensed that he was being well cared for.

About two weeks later I began having some very disturbing dreams. I seemed to be in some disjointed fashion, experiencing what Shane must have experienced during the car accident. While I seemed to be in the car, I had no control over it. I had the dream several times and though the scenario altered slightly each time the essence of the dream remained the same. I was terribly frightened. I felt as if Shane were trying to tell me something, though I could not be certain what. My ease of a few weeks ago vanished. I had read that sometimes when a soul departs the body suddenly, it often becomes confused and does not realize what has happened. They wander not knowing where they are, nor why they can not communicate. The thought that Shane might be caught between realities afraid and confused was almost more than I could bear. I began to pray more intensely than I had ever prayed in my entire life. I did not wish to infect the rest of the family with my fears. They had difficulties enough of their own. I begged, "Please God, can you just let me know, in whatever manner you see fit, that he is all right?" The plea was imparted constantly for days. On March 21 my answer came. I went to bed as usual. What follows I will classify as a dream because I do not know what other designation to give it so that you will understand. It was not, however, a dream in the accepted sense. I saw myself in bed. I heard a sound and sat up. I could see something standing in the doorway. The figure was very tall, taller than the doorway and clad entirely in white. As the form came through the doorway it became smaller. I could discern no face only the shape of a being dressed in white. As the apparition came into the room it became larger again, as if he were adjusting his size to fit the room. He came around the foot of my bed and I realized who he was, though I still could not distinguish a face. I could not seem to speak. I was very nervous and very excited. I understood even in this state that something unprecedented was happening and mentally warned myself if I did not speak I might never get another chance. I kept trying to force myself to speak, still, no sound came. Suddenly, he changed to the face and body which was familiar to me. Shane sat in a chair opposite me, His face radiantly beautiful with no evidence of scarring or injury. I reached out impulsively, taking both his hands in mine. I was not certain if I was supposed to, but I could not seem to restrain myself. There was a luminous transparency about his image as if he were made of light. I finally spoke saying emotionally, "I love you!" He smiled softly and the gesture seemed to fill the room with its radiance. Suddenly, he was sitting beside me on the bed. He did not get up and move, it was as if he thought about the action and it occurred. I was still holding both his hands. Not wanting to waste the opportunity I said, "Honey, do you understand what has happened?" He replied, "You mean about the accident? Yeah." At this point he began explaining what had happened and why. I am aware that I was told, though not specifically what I was told. The only detail I can remember is hearing him say, "We are going to feed them." The connection was broken suddenly as if someone had snapped his fingers and I found myself sitting in bed staring at the clock which read 2 A.M., the exact time of his death one month before.

I was very alert with a sense of serenity and elation completely unmatched by any other experience in my life. I realized that I had not just dreamed that he was present, I had been in his presence. By what means I was conveyed there I can not say. Aside from the fact that his image was sculpted from the most luminous exquisitely beautiful light, the most convincing aspect of the encounter was the fact that he was clean shaven. Since the age of sixteen Shane had worn a moustache. It was a part of his personality and very becoming. Had I conjured up the image, I would have done so with a moustache.

When Charlie arrived home from work an hour later I was still sitting up in bed completely captivated by the experience and anxious to tell him. He did not seem surprised, nor did my other children when I told them of my encounter. In fact, they replied that they had been waiting for me to make contact, knowing that if it were possible to reach Shane I would find a way. A doorway had opened for all of us, but with exactly what ramifications we could not yet be certain.

Shane had not been alone in the truck at the time of the accident. With him had been a friend Roger and Roger's girlfriend Julie. Roger had escaped injury, but Julie had been seriously injured and had been in the hospital in a nearby town for nearly a month. We had been very concerned about her and had visited her several times. We continued to correspond by mail after she had gone home from the hospital. We were concerned that while her physical injuries seemed to be mending, psychologically she was not healing well. Her mother reported that she was despondent, frightened of riding in cars particularly after dark, and could remember little about the accident. Several days after my encounter the phone rang. I answered to find Julie's mother on the line. She seemed very excited and anxious to tell me of Julie's progress. Something unusual had happened and she wanted to share it with me in the hope that I might find it comforting. Julie had, had a dream. In the dream Shane had come to her, encouraging her and telling her that she must get well. She must shake off the affects of the accident and help Roger to do the same. Her mother's voice choked with emotion as she related that Julie had been steadily improving since and was beginning to remember some of the details of the accident. I thanked her for letting me know, expressed our pleasure at Julie's improvement and told her that we, too, had been visited by Shane. These were only the first of many visits to each of us. Jennifer after going down stairs one night, came running back to say that she had seen Shane standing beside the doorway smiling at her. Chris and Marion reported on occasion seeing him visiting their home. Once I was sitting in the den reading. The house was quiet and I was alone. I glanced up and there on his favorite pillow sprawled out in front of the TV lay Shane. This was no transparent image but so realistic that I reached out to touch him. As I did so, he vanished. We all excitedly compared and discussed our encounters for several months. Gradually, however, they seemed to subside mostly into the dream state, and we were again faced with the reality of learning to live with only our memories to remind us.

David Shane Idol was born on August 10, 1986, five months after his father's death. At first there seemed to be no striking resemblance, then when he was five weeks old I spoke to him and he smiled. I saw Shane. The dimples, his father's dimples, were there in his cheeks after all and his smile held the same power to charm me as his father's had.

I realized now that for at least a year before Shane's death I had been carefully prepared so that when the blow fell I would not be completely crushed. I spent the next few months reflecting and analyzing details which I had not understood at the time. It was a quirk I had developed long ago and was, I suppose, an alternative to meditation. I had never been very successful with meditation, finding it virtually impossible to clear my mind for even fifteen minutes. I could focus intently on a particular question or problem but I did not posses the patience it took to clear my mind completely. Interestingly, it was one such attempt that I now pinpointed as the beginning of the preparation. The date was February 20, 1985 exactly one year before Shane's death. I had for some months had bits of lovely poetry floating through my mind from time to time. It always left me feeling very warm and loved. I carefully wrote each verse down and dated it (some examples may be found at the close of the chapters). When I was feeling depressed or down I took out the verses and read them. A high school teacher had instilled a love of poetry in me years ago, but my attempts at composing even the simplest verse were sadly inadequate. It was for this reason That I found this dictation so magical. I refer to it as dictation because that was how I felt at the time. I would feel a warm tingling sensation all over and the poetry would begin trailing through my mind. The same physical sensation always heralded the poetry. It continued for months and I was enchanted. I had no idea of the source. Since I needed to work on my meditation, I decided to meditate on the origin of the poetry. I laid down on the couch in the den quieted my mind and began trying to center my thoughts. The usual splotch of purple color appeared as I attempted to visualize with my mind's eye. As I concentrated on the even rhythm of my breathing the color was replaced by an eye, a single exquisitely beautiful eye. An eye which seemed to hold within its depths the secrets of infinity. For several moments I kept making attempts to visualize a pair of eyes but could never seem to clearly capture both. I was filled with a sense of calm well being that seemed to banish all thoughts of fear and apprehension. I asked mentally, "Who are you?" No answer came, only the steady unfathomable gaze of that solitary eye. After a few moments I asked again, "Who are you?" The reply was a single word, "Mirar" (the Spanish word meaning "to watch" or "contemplate"). The euphoria of the experience left me strangely quiet all day. I avoided telling anyone, for fear words would break the spell. I did as I was told. I watched and contemplated. A week or so later I came across a book entitled *The Power of Alpha Thinking* by Jess Stern. Since I had always had such difficulty meditating I decided to give alpha thinking a try. It seemed more interesting to me since the method involved the visualization of a quiet room in which one could contemplate whatever he chose. I was never able to make the room work to may satisfaction, though I kept trying. One day as I was attempting to furnish the room the location of the visualization changed spontaneously and I found myself walking along a beach. I decided, there after, to follow where I was led. I gave up trying to imagine the room and concentrated instead on the beach. The results were interesting. I found myself on that imaginary beach in a long flowing white robe. I reached down at my feet picked up a large sand dollar, turned toward the sea, held it heavenward and broke it open. Out flew a flock of white doves. Lying in the sand beside me, I saw a spool of silver cord. The cord had been cut. I had for some time prayed for a teacher, the symbol of which would be a single red rose. In the next exercise on the following day I was again walking along the beach when I was met by a dark-haired man with the most radiantly compelling eyes I have ever seen. He presented me with a single red rose. Each time I strolled along that mental beach I would turn and glance over my shoulder, seeing my footprints in the sand. These exercises continued successfully for nearly a year and had become the highlight of my day. They stopped abruptly two days before Shane's death. Reflecting back, I could see how much of the symbolism contained in those exercises dealt with future events. One of the most interesting occurred when the family returned home from the funeral services. Charlie handed me a card containing the minister's text for the ceremony. The service had centered around the poem, *Footprints*.

Each of us had been prepared in a manner that spoke uniquely to the individual. So much preparation. Was condolence its only object or were we slowly being drawn toward a deeper understanding?

It was December 23, 1987, twenty-two months after Shane's death. Charlie was working, Jennifer had gone to a party and I was alone. I am still not certain exactly how it came about. I was restless and plagued with a compelling feeling that someone was trying to communicate with me. I had never been successful at communication with other realities except within the dream state. I asked God to protect me from intrusion by unloving forces and for no reason which I can adequately explain relaxed, opening my being to whom ever it was who sought entry. I expected nothing more than my usual frustration with the silence. Suddenly, there appeared within my mind's eye trailers similar to ticker tapes containing words and letters. I was so startled that I missed the first few. I asked with whom I was communicating and the letters spelled out *Amazoz*. I noted aloud that the word spelled nothing in any language I understood and asked if there was an English equivalent. The letters spelled Shane. I felt the hair stand up on my arm and my mouth go dry, my flip attitude of a few moments before vanished. I repeated my question. The reply was the same. I said softly, "I love you." The letters spelled out, "I love you, too." I continued with some questions which I can no longer remember and asked in closing if I could speak with him again. The response was that "they" would be happy to speak with me again on December 24, at 9 P.M.

On Christmas Eve we celebrated with Charlie's family as had been our custom for many years, returning home at 9:10 P.M. I again relaxed, and opening my mind asked God's protection from anything unloving or harmful. I opened by addressing Shane and telling him how much I loved him. The movement of the letters was sluggish and erratic at first. When I asked why, the reply was, "You were late coming and we were waiting." In other words, please take this a little more seriously, we are not doing this for your amusement. My next question after the amenities was, "Who is WE?"

"WE", it seems, is a gathering of interested beings and a group which Shane refers to as "the wise ones". The wise ones are a council of exalted beings who possess an all-knowing wisdom and provide the answers which he could not. I was very eager and filled with questions. As the letters raced across my mind's eye I tried to tell the others the contents of the messages. I seemed to know, often before the spelling began, what would be said. This concerned me at first. I worried that I might be unconsciously manipulating the replies. After the second "session" as they came to be called, it was decided that someone should take down the answers because it was difficult to remember all that was said. At first the answers were short, sometimes only a few words. With practice the flow of information improved. Each session was held on Sunday evening at 9 P.M. and lasted for one hour. Charley was disturbed at first, fearing for my safety. I countered that so far the only messages which had come through were positive and loving. The moment there was a hint of anything else I would stop. I was always very careful in that respect. Both Shane and the Wise Ones warned repeatedly that this was no game and should not be used for the purpose of fortune telling. They spoke to us for the express purpose of sharing their wisdom with us, and reminded us continuously that this was a rare opportunity and should not be taken lightly. If we asked how we should proceed in certain circumstances, we were advised that they could not make decisions for us, we must learn our own lessons and make our own choices. They were allowed to encourage, lovingly support, and in some cases advise, but they could never make decisions for us. There was certain information which they were not allowed to convey, either because we were not ready to know, or because knowing might influence some future decision. We were encouraged in all circumstances to respond lovingly to others.

We asked many questions of Shane, concerning his welfare, how he was adjusting, what his environment was like and found his answers to be very comforting. He informed us that his soul, upon departing the body, "flew straight to the Father." I asked if his experience was similar to the near death experiences which I had read about. He replied that it was not. I asked how his experience was different. "They were *near* death experiences," he stated, and explained that with death there are no barriers. I questioned him about how he appeared to us. Again he patiently explained that he did not "appear," but rather, he triggered the mental suggestion of his presence and we in turn mentally produced the image. Many of the concepts were difficult to understand at first. For instance, when we referred to seeing him in dreams he repeatedly corrected us by saying, "You do not dream." This was difficult to grasp even though it was explained that dreaming was more a state of mind used for problem solving or sometimes purely for entertainment. The closest thing I could come up with that paralleled this state of mind was a holographic situation created out of one's subconscious into which he could step and become an integral part of temporarily, working with scenarios which aided his understanding.

After a month or so it became apparent that our method of communication was slow and clumsy. I asked if there was a more efficient way to communicate. They answered that we could try recording. So, on another night at a prearranged time I was told to ask a question let the tape recorder run and listen for the answer. I did as instructed but there was never any sound on the tape. They encouraged me to keep trying.

The session beginning on the seventh or eighth Sunday was different. I sensed it immediately. I felt a quickening sensation, a warm tingling through out my entire body, much the same as I had felt when the poetry was conveyed. For the first time I was frightened and ready to back out. I addressed Shane and asked for an explanation. He reassured me, asked me to be calm and told me that someone else would be taking over the communication. He explained that He was a very enlightened and very loving being, one who was completely compatible with my life force, and because of this, communication would be made considerably easier. I was not certain I was comfortable with this at all! Talking to Shane was one thing, I completely trusted him, but this. I was not at all certain that I wanted to continue. Shane begged for my trust, assuring me that I would be loved and protected at all times. They had a great deal of information to convey and this communication link was the most compatible available and would be much more rewarding. Shane promised that I would still be allowed to speak with him each week and that he would always be present. Hesitantly, I greeted the new communicator and asked his name. He replied, "You may address me as My Lord." The communication was definitely more distinct and finally I understood how they intended me to use the tape recorder. I was to ask my questions, listen for the reply in my mind and repeat what was said into the tape recorder. I felt rather foolish when I recalled how I had expected them to create a voice on the tape. I realized now that was not possible. Ours was a mind link. After that, the communication improved immensely. The answers lengthened, becoming more sophisticated. It seemed to flow spontaneously from my mind without any effort on my part. Finally, I had exhausted my list of questions, but still felt that I had not even begun to touch on the information they wished to convey. I asked if they could suggest some questions that I might ask which would draw out the desired information. For the next two years they dictated both the questions and the answers. They identified themselves as The Brotherhood of Raphael, those who are charged by the Father with the bringing of the light.

I share with you their wisdom and pray you find it as enlightening, loving, and spiritually awakening as I have.

What of the caterpillar
who spends its entire life
in self gratification and
in its final act of decadence
spins for itself a silken shroud.
Like all living things,
only in its dying does it
reach its full potential.
It emerges at the appointed
time from its pseudo prison,
carrying within the gossamer
beauty of its wings
the secret mysteries of the soul.
                    (11/12/87)

CHAPTER VI

GOD, OUR FATHER

I don't think there is one of us who has not in some deep fit of depression lain in the darkest corner of his being, asking is God really there? Does He love me? If so why does He allow such terrible things to happen to me? Am I such a bad person that He has abandoned me? Why doesn't He hear me when I call Him for help?

They began with the basics:

"You are a child of God. When at your most selfless you are an exquisitely beautiful creature. Unencumbered by the body you are a radiant being of light with love and beauty genetically inherent within you. If you will permit, we wish to tell you of your Father, your true nature, your lineage, your true home, and your heritage.

"Your Father is an omnipotent force of love and power completely devoid of guile, anger, hatred, or any negative aspect. The Father's mind is the spirit of giving, love, and selflessness. As your soul evolves it nears oneness with Him, The ultimate union, much sought after by all the souls who occupy infinity.

"You are body mind, and spirit a perfect mirror of God and created in His image. You are all these things, but your spirit is the only aspect of your nature which survives throughout eternity. The body and mind are expressions of the spirit. The spirit is holy, never dies, and shall be one with God. God is within each of you, coaxing you toward a more loving nature. Your intellect can encompass infinity through the Father. For when you allow Him in, you tap the universal mind and the source of all that is, leaving no more enigmas to question.

"All life reflects the Father. Some reflections are more loving than others, however. All worlds end with recognition of Him. Immediately upon departing the body, you are aware of His

65

glorious presence and the love which emanates from it. It is something you can not fully experience within the body. The body is deceptive. It draws so much attention to itself, allowing one to forget his source. However, when the body loses its usefulness, causing the spirit to seek its source, it perceives the Father. For it is out of His love the soul is born and it is to His love that it shall return. The love of God is all encompassing, all forgiving, and unconditional. He loves each of you as if you were the only one.

"You are the motivator of the material world and when in contact with another have the potential of being God's messenger. You have yet to reach your true potential by fully expressing your own beauty and the image of God within you. You are upon the Earth to express God and to change your habitat into an expression of love. You are an extension of your creator and everything you are and hope to be relates to Him. Your life here is an opportunity for you to conquer the limitations and material aspects of your nature. You consider Earth the ultimate expression of life, when in actuality the ultimate expression of life lies beyond.

"The Father is the center of the cosmos, the source of all that is. Everything radiates outward from Him. Without the Father there is nothingness. He thinks and it is. It is His wish that you understand why it is so. He is at the center of every cell and microcosm in infinity. He gives to you His most precious gift, a portion of Himself. Your soul is a reflection of the Father and you can not escape who you are, though you may deny it through countless lives, punishing yourself needlessly. Listen to the small voice inside yourself, the one you think is your own mind. It is the voice of your Father asking to love you. Love is everything, the union which unites us all. It cures all ills, binds all wounds, solves all problems. If you can learn to love, only to love, it will solve everything that is wrong with you and your world. Love is the only thing that matters. If life has not love, then it is no longer life. Love attracts, reflects, and creates love. It revolves continuously, returning over and over to its source who is the center of everything."

It seemed and over simplification to me that an omnipotent God with the power to control infinity would say if you just love everything will be alright. Patiently, they continued:

"All are one in the Father's love and one is all. It is a beautiful paradox that you can be one and you can be all at the same time. God is one, He is all, and all is love. You can not imagine the power love holds. It is more powerful than anything of which you are aware.

"You and your brother contain equal amounts of the Father. Respect your brother's essence and the reflection of God within him. Never turn from love nor extend your fist in anger. Hold out your hand in love with your heart in it. Then you will see the reflection of the Father, for it will return to you in the mirror of your own action. God sees into the hearts of all. He is able to see all of one's heart, mind, and potential which has come down through many lives. He is aware of each man's reasons for being upon the Earth, the lessons he is here to learn, and what lies ahead upon his path. You will always be a part of him, whether you choose to acknowledge it or not. You can not escape. You can not run, nor can you hide. It is always there with you. This gift of love is to sustain you through whatever havoc you wreak upon yourselves. You have but to look within. He knows each of you better than you know yourselves. He knows your strengths, weaknesses, and capabilities."

Interesting, I mused, but why are we kept in the dark. Wouldn't man be more responsive if he knew what to expect? They mentally sighed, took a deep breath, and continued:

"To those who have a willingness to hear, the knowledge will be provided. You are often confused by the trickery of the place which you inhabit. The vibrations of the Earth plane are designed to confuse and trick you into believing that it is reality. You must understand that what you are seeing is subjective. It deceives you, causing you to forget who you are. You react to the Earth as though it were your home. It is not. It is an illusion. Your home is elsewhere and is more beautiful than anything of which you can conceive."

They continued in the vein which they had begun before I interrupted:

"All God's children carry His mark, a mark of love which emanates from your presence. You can not hide it, nor can you disguise it. It is the touch of the Father's mind upon your spirit. You earn His mark by loving. It shines from your being and is easily recognizable by others. You have but to look into the eyes of another to see the mirror of God reflected there. One may be able to disguise his physical appearance or school his facial expressions, but he can not disguise his eyes. There you will see the true reflection of the soul within."

It was difficult to imagine some of the people I had encountered carrying the mark of God. Was it possible that I just did not have the vision with which to see, or know where to look? I could tell they were relieved that I had finally realized it.

"You will find the answers you seek within," they continued. "You look outside yourself and find more of the same. You can not find what you desire or what will quench your thirst and sustain you, outwardly. 'I am here,' is the Father's message, 'I have brought love enough so that each of you might have his portion. It is yours, freely given and without condition. You have but to take it.' You need wander no longer seeking love. It is within you as it has been all along. The Father has waited patiently, allowing you to stretch, grow, and learn. He has given you the opportunity to experience all that the Earth has to teach you. The time has come for that experience and knowledge to be used, creating the essence which God intended from the beginning. You were intended to be a being of love and selflessness. He did not wish that you should be separate one from the other, with separate religions, races, languages, and sexes. It is His wish that all of you be brothers and share in His love. You beg, 'Father Help me'. Yet, You turn from those who are sent, distrusting their motives. You have no cause to fear. What is it you fear, my children, love, light, life? There is only you and I and the love that we share.

"You will eventually realize who you are and what your relationship to the Father is. It may take some longer than others, but in due time all shall understand. You have difficulty believing that the Father truly loves you. It troubles Him to see you in pain with such feelings of unworthiness. You distress yourselves needlessly. You need not do anything to earn His love and it will cost you nothing. You are His child. That is enough. Sit quietly and listen to the voices of your mind. Harken to the longings of your heart. You long for something this world does not possess. If you could be satisfied within this world you would have found satisfaction already. You have searched everywhere. You have searched the highest mountain and the deepest sea. You have sought satisfaction in money and power and found little solace. All the while what you sought lies within you. All the divine knowledge which you scour the great books to find, all which is sought within scientific calculations and complex problems find their answers within you, my children. The Father provides all that you need, only you seek it in the wrong place. You have but to listen to that still small voice within and the wisdom of the ages will be revealed to you. You shall finally understand the reality, that you were dead and now shall live."

I could feel the warmth beginning to surge within me. Was it possible that God loved me, just as I am, for no apparent reason than just to love me? I, too, have responsibilities I learned.

"You must release your petty anger and resentment and understand that the only answer is love. Love is contagious and loving yourself is the first step toward loving your brother. Love must include forgiveness. You can not love without first forgiving. Each of you, no matter how insignificant you consider yourself to be, is an equal part of the Father. Within your heart is the remembrance of the true nature of the Father. You have allowed yourself to be tricked by your environment into believing that the Father is some far distant being who is never pleased with you. This is not your Father. Your Father is love itself and you, my children, are heir to that love. He knows that eventually you will respond to the whispers and inner prompting and acknowledge your true nature."

Funny, I had always sort of taken love for granted, forgetting that virtually everything subsisted and flourished with a steady diet of love.

"Love increases the Father who is the source of all love. It is the only thing which multiplies when it is given away, increasing as each of you receive and give love. It goes out in ever expanding circles and comes back in on itself, only to reverberate outward again. You can not hide nor contain love, for if you do it shrivels and dies. If love is to survive it must spread outward. The process is repeated until every single soul has known and experienced love."

Anyone who has read the bible or studied any doctrine has encountered continuous, often times, mysterious references to the light. Light, air, food, now love were the necessities of life, but there was more...

"The light is the mind of God shining inside you. It illumines everything with its beautiful aura. It radiates from the mind of God outward in tiny pinpoints of brilliance which reflect off everything that is encountered. The light is the holy wisdom of God, penetrating into the mind and heart of man so that he may see and understand all that the Father is, was, and ever shall be. The Father and the Christ are one and fill all of infinity with their eternal presence. Each time a soul returns to the Father, the light increases and makes the glowing circle larger and wider to encompass more and more. It will continue to expand, illuminating every single heart until none are left dark and fearful. In this manner all God's children may possess the light, accepting their heritage as His child. It carries within it the beauty of His love and the understanding of His holy purpose. You can avail yourself of the light, but you must understand that only love will summon the light. Life, love, and the light are one. They are combined and made manifest within the Father and reside within each of you who are made in His image. Open your being and allow them to shine forth for all to see. The light nourishes growth and beauty and contains all truth for there are no shadows in which to hide untruth. It illuminates all minds and shares its reality with all who are willing to see. The Christ showed you by the example of His holy being that with selfless love you may step into the light and become one with it just as He did. Look into the light and you shall see the face of God. All fear will be subjected to the scrutiny of the light, for when examined in the light, fear dissolves."

This all sounded beautiful, wonderful, but there seemed to be little reflection of the light within our world today and trying to expose what was there often subjected one to severe reproach.

"The Christ knows and understands the problems you face while occupying the body and how difficult your world is," they replied. "In overcoming the body, He endeavored to help you to understand that you can overcome it as well. Step into the light and allow it to illumine your being, then you, too, may conquer the illusions of your world. You were once aware of the truth concerning the Father, but you allowed the Earth to obscure your vision of what lies beyond. You have come to believe that belief, in a world of limitless love and beauty are only vague imaginings or wishful thinking. You have difficulty seeing beyond the fantasy created by your plane. At the outer edges of your world are the beginnings of the light. If you could but allow tiny pin holes of it to enter the darkness, then you would soon open the door which leads through to the other side and into the presence of the Father.

"You are aware only of what others have told you of the Christ. You have heard of the miracles and healing. You listen to His teachings but do not truly hear, nor understand. You find His ability to raise someone from the dead extraordinary, however, the miracles which the Master wrought took little of His power. He has the power to command life, death, and infinity. You, knowing little of Him, have been impressed with parlor tricks, while completely missing the beauty of the love and the radiance of the light which flowed from His holy being. You saw little of this, nor were you particularly impressed by the fact that He could love even those who tortured Him. It is a pity that your vision is so limited. Love and gentleness are strong, while anger, hatred, and fear are weak. It is the Father's hope that you will eventually come to prefer love and beauty to anger and hatred."

I had always understood the uniqueness of the Christ, but He was with the Father. Those left to carry on for Him had long since departed, as well. Meanwhile, our Earth seemed to continually deteriorate into the blackness of despair. What were we to do?

"There are certain beings whom God chose at the beginning, implanting within their hearts and minds the beauty of His love along with the master plan to return man to his rightful place," they assured. " They bear the imprint of the Father's mind upon theirs. They are not compelled by man, only by the Father. They hear His voice within their heart, feel His direction in their lives, and respond by spreading the light to all whom they encounter. They have a glow about them, a warmth, and a feeling of welcome which beckons to others. There is a feeling of trust which indicates they will neither harm you, nor try to suppress your own natural beauty. You may recognize them by their willingness to accept you as you are simply because you are their brother. He chose very special beings with a great capacity to love and the ability to accept the failings and inadequacies of others while still responding with love. They appear much the same as other men but at the core of their being is the light and love of His own heart. It is difficult to look upon one of these and not realize that there is something unique about them. It often appears as an intangible quality, an inner radiance which is projected outward. Only the Father is wise enough to choose those who will be sent. Only He knows who will nourish the love and light and offer it to their brothers. Only He sees into the hearts of all, knowing which are fertile enough to plant the seeds of love. Only He knows who will not grow faint or weary and which will remain faithful to the tasks appointed them. Their radiance can not be disguised. Their behavior toward their brothers, their interest, caring, and willingness to share the truth they bear with others, all bear testament to their relationship to God. You recognize that certain individuals seem to command the Father's attention and find it mysterious and supernatural. It is merely love. If you have been chosen you are confident of His love for you and know instinctively that when you turn to Him your needs will be met. You recognize the sound of His voice and trust it above all others. It matters little whether other men believe, for you are attuned only to His voice within your heart."

CHAPTER VII

LIFE AFTER DEATH

What was it like to die, I wondered. The thought of death seems to automatically invoke fear. I had personally faced the grim specter of death; had felt the crushing agony of losing my beloved children to its clutches. Death and dying were different, this I understood. I knew something of dying, but little of death. They set about correcting that deficiency.

"Upon leaving the body, you are suddenly free to fly the universe and soar upward toward the Father. There is a complete lack of fear, a need only to respond, to feel, and to be. You are a part of the light, as well as a network of love which goes on for infinity. It is not a visual sensation, but one that permeates your entire being. Your chains are gone and with them the pain of confinement. You can not understand why you found the body so attractive. Standing in the light, you are consumed with utter bliss. Your soul is aware instantly of the light and the Father's love. It flies on wings of anticipation toward Him, soaring upward in spirals of joy with the sheer delight of being free. You revel in the acuteness of the color, music, and light which is present. You sense that within that glorious light lies what your soul has sought since its conception."

I remembered fondly Shane's exclamation that it was great not having to "mess" with that body.

"Until you are free of the body, your awareness is limited. You can not comprehend the soul's compulsion toward oneness with the Father, for you see Him as a distant force somewhere within a remote corner of the vastness of infinity. He is inside you, as He has always been. The Father's world is very different from the world you occupy. Your world is one of things which you must touch or see in order to believe. In your world one has little faith in things he can not prove. In the world beyond you have but to think and it is. It is a world of concepts and there are no barriers other than those which you erect to separate you from complete love, happiness, and beauty. All is yours for the taking. Nothing inhibits you but your own thoughts and lack of vision. When your thoughts are free, then whatever you believe can be. You become one with all that is. Your brothers who are already free are there to greet you. They guide you, providing all that you need. You find, however, that you desire only love and they give it abundantly. It is as if you have spent your entire life locked in a musty little closet with no light. Suddenly, someone opens the door, releasing you so that you may see the beautiful world which exists outside the closet."

Their dissertation evoked parallels of Socrates' *Allegory of the Cave*.

"The light of God, you discover, fills all of infinity. It is not light as you are used to seeing from a light bulb, or even the sun which illuminates your entire planet. The light of the Father radiates throughout all life and knows no limits. It can not be quenched, hidden, nor contained. His light is large enough to encompass all that is and small enough to fit within each man's heart.

"After the limited confinement of the body you must reacclimate yourself to a world of limitless possibilities. You must discern the level of your ability to love. The Nation of the Dead is a test which every soul must experience upon entering the Father's kingdom. You must view the image of yourself as you really are. Without the body to obscure your vision, you can no longer hide. You see not only who you are, but what you have become. Some do not find the sight pleasant, nor understand that they are seeing themselves. They believe they are seeing demons and believe themselves to be in Hell. All you are perceiving, however, is what is inside you without the body to disguise your inner being."

This seemed confirmation of judgment, though, I was to find quite different from what I had always believed.

"Take care the thoughts and feelings you store deep within yourself. Do not hold onto pettiness, hatred, and anger. It is not pleasant to see yourself in this way. If ugliness and anger are what you store inside, then these are the things you shall see.

"The Christ is there to help you with your transition through the World (Nation) of the Dead. His is the light which serves as a beacon to guide you through this dark place. He remains near you so that you may feel His love, encouraging you to be strong and unafraid. He and all those who come to greet you, constantly send love and prayers for your safe passage. You are not hopelessly trapped, as many feel. You may release yourself from the World of the Dead by desiring to be released. You have but to think and it occurs. Understanding that your thoughts instantly manifest themselves, is a part of the acclimation into the Father's kingdom. You may simply think, 'I do not like this place and wish to leave it.' As the thought occurs to you, you are released. You see, everything beyond the body is controlled by thought. It is for this reason that it is so important to rid yourself of anger before you depart the body. Anger binds and holds you to all that is ugly and unpleasant. Desiring love will draw it to you, being angry that you do not have love will keep you from it. Remember, anger only breeds anger and hatred only breeds hatred. Like attracts like. It is for this reason that love is so important. Love spreads outward in ever widening circles to include all that is. Love sets you free. Anger traps you and will not let you go."

I had puzzled my entire life over Christ's admonition that anger put one in danger of the judgment. Anger is an emotion virtually everyone has suffered at one time or another. It flared quickly and was just as quickly gone, seemingly...

"When one's anger traps him within the Nation of the Dead, the Father mercifully allows His child to "sleep" until he can set aside his ire and remember that there is no place for it within the Father's world."

At this point I interrupted to ask about a term they had used so frequently. In our world "sleep" was either a means of rest or, in the case of animals a colloquialism denoting euthanasia. What, I wanted to know, did the "sleep" of which they spoke entail.

"Sleep within the Father's kingdom," they replied, "is a state akin to your understanding of suspended animation, though slightly different because there is no body to contend with. When the soul has been shocked or deeply disoriented by his transition, or his experience within the Nation of the Dead to the point that he has difficulty coping with and reacclimating to the Father's kingdom, then he must be remanded to a state in which there is no responsibility, or awareness. There is nothing in this state to distress the soul further until he has healed. He is cared for tenderly and nurtured lovingly by the gentlest of beings who are experienced in these matter. When one is able to cope and resume his duties he awakens and is guided carefully back into the mainstream of life again. Many times a soul comes through the Nation of the Dead successfully, but finds the journey arduous and very tiring. Being in need of a brief respite, He may take a 'nap' and sleep for a short period."

I asked how a soul was awakened and what indicators were used to signify that a soul had recovered sufficiently. They replied that a soul was aware within themselves when they were able to resume and spontaneously awakened. I wondered how long one usually slept in such cases.

"There is no set time limit," they replied, "some remain in this state for a short while, some for thousands of years as you discern time. It depends on the individual. One is never measured by the standards of another, but is allowed to progress at his own pace. Prayers are very helpful for those who sleep, for in this state the only thing which they can assimilate is love."

I must confess that I found this somewhat disquieting at first and asked how one could avoid this situation.

"If you are afraid and call upon the Father begging, 'Father, please help me, then you are instantly released.' If you have become accustomed to calling upon Him when in need, then it will be second nature to do so within the Nation of the Dead. If you have learned to meet each challenge with anger and defiance, thinking you need help from no one, then you will trap yourself. In such instances there is no solution other than to 'sleep' until your anger dissipates.

"You are often repelled by those you encounter within the Nation of the Dead, not realizing that you only encounter aspects of yourself there. The only ugliness and demons you will see are those which exist within you. You must confront all which has lain hidden beneath the facade of the body. If you have not provided fertile ground for discord and antagonism within, then you shall not see any. You shall see only what is within you!

"You pay your own debts and are not held accountable for the obligations of another. You only encounter you own rancor. If you see repulsive images, they are images put there by your own refusal to respond lovingly. Remember, if you release your anger and seek to retain only love, then the images you see upon encountering yourself will reflect that effort."

My Mother passed away a little over a year after Shane's death. She was a fiercely independent person and was forced by the nature of her illness to be confined to a nursing home. She died very angry and resentful. I remember one night in the dream state being allowed to see what she had seen while viewing her anger. Words can not adequately explain the horror. After that I was able to appreciate the merciful balm of "sleep" and the calamity of anger.

"Your crowning achievement, upon departing the body, is realizing the legacy of love and beauty which await you," they resumed. "You have learned your lessons well, which entitles you to be a part of a vast brotherhood of love and light in which you are taught with patience and love. The vastness of the world of which you have become a part boggles the mind. It is a world filled with beauty and love. You are home!

"There are those within the Father's kingdom whose job it is to ease your transition from the material body to your natural state. The sole purpose of these beings is to help you to adjust to the changes you find there and the aspects which are unfamiliar to you. You are prepared long before the time of your departure so that the adjustment will occur as smoothly as possible."

It is only with hindsight and much reflection that I came to the realization that Shane knew he was going to die. The kinds of questions he asked of me and the things he said indicated to me that he was getting his house in order. His Dad and I differ on whether he consciously knew, or just had a feeling that there was to be a momentous change for him. Regardless of which is true, he was aware on some level that he was about to depart the body. It is a comfort to know that he was surrounded by those who cared for him as much as I did.

"The Father has no wish to crush His children," they assured me. "He does everything possible to make the transition easier for you. It is only when you fight His love and refuse His help that difficulties arise. He will not force His help upon you. It is freely given, but it must be freely accepted, as well. We understand that you have been confined and the adjustment to freedom can sometimes be difficult. Occasionally, a spirit who comes to freedom too quickly uses it foolishly and creates difficulties for himself. You must be properly conditioned and conducted so that you will not waste the opportunities which are available. God loves you. He will not simply throw you out the door and off a cliff to fend for yourself. He wants to help you, to guide you, and those who have experienced His love are there for that purpose."

Once when they were discussing the consequences of anger I asked what happened if one was afraid. They replied that fear is a natural reaction to things which are unfamiliar.

"Those who are frightened of being released from the body are helped to understand that the body is a learning tool and they no longer require its confinement. They are helped to accept that the body is, after all, only a thought form, something created by the soul so that it might grasp things which can be experienced in no other way. They are helped to realize that they no longer need the things which this particular body can offer and that the time has arrived to evaluate what has been learned and incorporate it into their being so that it may be used for the benefit of the soul. Sometimes it is a difficult process. Some find it difficult to sever the ties and attachments of the body and find themselves simply wandering, seeking entry into the body again. When this occurs, the Father mercifully allows them to 'sleep.'

"When you are set free to learn and experience on your own it may seem overwhelming at first so one is carefully guided. This new-found freedom is not frightening to most, however, only different and more expansive. You become reacquainted with old familiar friends and enjoy liberties which are not possible while confined within the limitations of the material world. Within the Father's world you are one with all that is.

"After one has concluded his journey through the Nation of the Dead, He is taken into the company of a group of wise ones and allowed to review all the events of his past sojourn within the body to assess what has been learned. During this evaluation, one is guided step by step with the help of very loving beings through each phase of his life to see how loving he has been and how well he has taken advantage of the opportunities for learning available to him."

When Shane had mentioned this aspect to me, I kept questioning him about his appearance before this group. He corrected my use of the term appear by reminding me that there is no physical manifestation within the Father's world. One of the first things I learned in these conversations was that the terms must be specific in order for the questions to be answered correctly. It is also wise to be certain that you are ready to accept the exact truth because artifice is not among their capabilities.

I asked about those left behind.

"When discarding the body, one regrets leaving his loved ones. Parting with those he has grown close to and come to love, is often difficult, but he responds to an even greater love. Loved ones are not forsaken, only separated for a time to be rejoined later. Once you have loved someone you continue to be a part of them and they of you. Once love is given it remains and continues to grow forever. The soul is soon busy with its studies and duties here and has little time to waste in nostalgia. Do not grieve for those who precede you into the Father's world. They are waiting for you to join them and share in their love. We feel compassion for those left behind. We are aware of your sorrow and mourn your misunderstanding of the event which you call death. What has occurred for us is the loveliest, most beautiful thing possible for a soul. To be with the Father is unmatched in beauty, love, and joy. We have not ceased to be, but have simply gone to a higher level. We have departed our shell because it is no longer necessary. Most beings leave of their own accord at a time they themselves have designated."

This was a totally new concept for me. A being actually chose the time and, oftentimes, manner of their own departure before birth.

"You must give up your sorrow and your fear of their departure long enough to realize that they continue. They are free, happy, and whole again. They live more fully now than when within the body. They are not dead. Dead is when one no longer remembers who he is, what his connection to the Father is, what he is to do, and how he is to do it. This state of unknowing is actually the situation when one is within the body and what *we* refer to as death. We are alive, free to love, live and be one with the Father," they assured me. "It is we who grieve for you when we are free of the body, for we realize that you are still entrapped and limited in your experience. We pray for your awakening."

It was at this point that I had my first experience with perceiving a concept. In light of all they had said I was contemplating my true identity. Suddenly, somewhere within my consciousness, a window opened briefly and I saw my soul as it is when completely unfettered by the body. A verbal description is difficult. Some things simply defy language. The aspects of which I was most aware, however, were that the soul is androgynous and completely limitless. It is a vast collection of light particles, carrying with them the genetic makeup of the Father. Needless to say, I understood why they considered those within the body dead.

"Communication with departed loved ones is not only possible, but quite simple really," they informed me. "The qualities which you found beautiful, loving, and endearing in one while they occupied the body survives for all infinity. In essence one is the same being you knew within the body, they have simply sloughed off the shell which confined them. You may communicate anytime you wish simply by quieting your mind and allowing it to respond. Even if your loved one is asleep you may pray for him, sending him your love. He will experience your love and it will help him to awaken. In many cases loved ones may appear briefly to reassure you of their well being. The departed soul uses your thought process to create an illusory visual image, one which you can identify and more easily commune with because the form is familiar to you. The recipient must be one who is sensitive to the broader realities of life and able to expand his mind beyond the confines of this plane. Often, a deep love for another will create an acute sensitivity, enabling one to create this phenomenon. Some are sensitive enough to produce these images quite easily. Within the dream state these occur quite effortlessly, but within what you call the waking state it is sometimes more difficult. One must be very tranquil, allowing his mind to be flexible so that it may reach beyond what seems to be toward what really is.

"When one of your brothers departs the body rejoice that he is free. Free from his confinement. Free to experience the Father, the Master, their love and the light which surrounds them. We realize that your vision is limited within the body and we are trying to help you to see the light. You have begun to understand a little. In some cases, such as the very old, or when one's body is very ill, causing them great pain, you do not lament quite so much at their departure. You must understand, however, that all who leave the body, regardless of their chronological age, are free and leave by their own choosing!"

In the beginning, before God allowed me to see Shane and talk with him, the one thing I could not even bear to think of was that he might not have died instantly. Thinking of him lying there, in pain, was more than I could bear. When we asked for a closed casket, the mortician replied, "That is probably best. I don't have anyone who can make him look the way he once did." Only God, at the moment of death, had the ability to make him more beautiful than before.

"No pain or physical impairment remains after the physical death of the body," they confirmed. "Pain is a physical sensation and the instant one leaves the body he is restored to his natural state and pain is no more. The only thing which brings distress to the discarnate soul is the inability to overcome anger, hatred, and jealousy. Even then the Father is merciful and allows sleep. No soul is ever tormented by the Father or by any within His kingdom! Any torment which you experience is of your own making.

"To those of you who grieve the Father is compassionate and will not send you more than you are able to bear. He has no wish to burden you beyond your capacity to endure. You are not separated from your loved ones as punishment, nor does God take them from you. When One has learned all he can from a body, he departs and this is as it should be. It would be cruel of the

Father to force him to stay longer. You grieve for nothing. Rejoice, your loved one is home, experiencing peace, joy and love.

"There are no accidents and there are no miracles."

This particular concept I still wrestle with on occasion.

"There is no way in which you can prevent one's departure when the time has come. Indeed, you should not wish to do so, for you confine and imprison them when you try. A soul was meant to be free. You must allow them their freedom and release them to their destiny. Send them with your blessings and love. When you have learned your lessons, you, too, shall be free.

"If you feel the presence of a loved one who has departed you are truly blessed."

This I can attest to.

"Few who are within the Earth plane welcome their departed brothers with joy. Relinquish your fear, for nothing separates you except the barriers which you erect. Prayer for the departed is essential. Do not worry that your prayers are not eloquent. When you reach out in prayer, the Father gathers you into His arms and provides whatever you need. It is the reaching out which is important, because He is already aware of your needs before you ask. You will encounter your loved ones again, for we shall all be a part of the Father again. There is no need for you to question. Nothing ever dies. No one ever dies! When you love someone you are drawn to them instinctively. If you have ever loved in the existence of your soul, you are drawn again to the object of that love. You can not be separated from those you love. Your very love binds you. You believe in something which does not exist. You mourn phantoms. You flail yourself and heap ashes upon your head, tormenting yourself needlessly! DEATH DOES NOT EXIST! No one ever ceases to be. The Father salvages something of every single being. The more you expand the love within you, the more of your being will continue to be.

"From the moment you depart your body, the Master is at your side, keeping you constantly in the halo of His holy light. The light is always in front of you to guide you. If you are incapable of finding the light He will show you. Your loved ones accompany Him so that you might recognize someone familiar. You are reassured by their presence and understand the fallacy of your belief in the torment of death, for there is only joy and beauty within them now."

I asked how much time was required for acclamation into the Father's world.

"The length of the adjustment period depends upon the individual," they stated. "If a being is highly evolved there is virtually no adjustment at all, for they know instantly upon leaving the body their destination, their goal, and what awaits them. Some who are less evolved experience some difficulty in adjusting and their surroundings are not quite so familiar to them. They are more attached to the body and do not wish to leave it behind. The world outside the body is very different from the world within the body. Your world is very limited. Everything which is perceived is but a pale image of reality. The body limits your senses, your means of expression, your perceptions and thought. Life outside the body is limitless and boundless. You can express yourself in anyway you choose. All means of expression are beautiful, loving, and joyous with no fear of reprimand. The Father enjoys the individuality and creativity of His children and would in no way repress their unique abilities. While within the Earth plane you establish little boundaries which limit everything. Outside the body the only boundaries are those you choose to recognize. You are free to share all that you are and hope to be without fear of rebuke. Within the Father's kingdom you should not expect to feel the same sensations you feel while in the body. The senses are far more intense and acute. One's intellect is unlimited for the Father's world is one of thought and whatever you can conceive, you can create. It is prudent while within the body to begin learning to control your thoughts, for a power so great can cause some difficulty if it is undisciplined. Think positively. If you ponder frightening evil thoughts excessively, then upon departing the body, these thoughts will manifest and cause you a great deal of unnecessary distress."

They quickly segued into a discussion on our ideas and misconceptions of Heaven and Hell.

"You believe the place you call heaven to be far away and do not truly understand the concept. You think in terms of the planet Earth. You envision an opulent city with golden streets, buildings of white marble, palaces of grand proportions with jewels and all the material treasures which you consider important. Material things do not concern the Father. Why should He build a city of material things when these things can be produced so easily by anyone with a thought? These elements which you consider valuable are used as a standard in your literature so that you can obtain some concept of the value of what you seek. God's world is a realm of the heart, mind, and spirit and has nothing to do with anything which is of a material nature. One does not travel far to this place you call Heaven, for it is within you. It is a state of being. A state of utter joy and love which all may experience. When you can reach a level at which you can let go of everything except love, then all the Father's realm throughout infinity will be yours. The 'places' Heaven and Hell exist as material realities only if you choose to create them for yourself. There is no pit of fire into which the Father casts His children. He loves you and does everything possible to spare you pain. All of the pain you feel was created by your negative response to love. The state you refer to as heaven is composed of a glorious collective resource of love which grows each time you love another. Hell is a fabrication which man created to explain the force of evil which accumulates when one refuses to love his brother. Love is more powerful than evil. If you continue to nourish the source of love, then evil will be eradicated. The 'places' Heaven and Hell exist only within your mind and have no power other than that which you give to them. If you wish to create a Heaven then banish all thoughts of Hell from your mind. Refuse to even acknowledge its existence. Acknowledge only love and soon your world will be filled with things which reflect your thoughts and attitudes."

They again took up what one may experience upon departing the body and introduced the subject of enlightened beings.

"Most enlightened beings are aware of what to expect upon departing the body and fly instantly to the Father. They sense that they have been away only briefly and experience joy at returning home again. Those who are less enlightened may be slightly confused at first, for they assumed that death was quite different. Initially, they do not realize that anything unusual has happened. They often believe that they have slept and awakened to this lovely place. They can not understand why those around them do not respond. They try to communicate with those still within the body, not realizing that they have departed. Loving beings are sent, often accompanied by a departed loved one who is familiar to them, to clear their confusion. They watch over you constantly, for they are charged never to relinquish or misplace any of the Father's children. You must, however, allow them to help you. They will not force their will upon you. All within God's world is freely given, but subject to the innate right to the free will of the individual. Recognition of loved ones who preceded you from the body will be automatic. You can always sense the presence of those you love. The physical and mental barriers of the body are necessary so that you can concentrate on your lessons. Choices are given, and one must choose without interference or without referring to the past or future. A choice must be made to respond lovingly in all things with only the aid of immediate references. Knowing the consequences of a particular decision, would require no learning on your part. The gift of hind sight and foresight are often removed in order that you might learn to choose with care and understand that every choice has a consequence. You must learn that nothing is without purpose. So, choose lovingly in all that you do so that the outgrowth of your decisions will be stepping stones rather than stumbling blocks. Seek the Father's counsel within yourself. It will provide the guidance you need and wise choices will become natural for you."

CHAPTER VIII

THE EDUCATION OF A SOUL

I could never resign myself to the belief that this life we lead and struggle with is a haphazard crazy quilt of pieces strewn together with no thought, no plan, no meaning. I always thought of it as a giant puzzle and if one could think deeply enough and reason clearly enough the pieces could be put together. I suppose I was actually struggling to remember. Listening to these taped messages began the long pilgrimage toward understanding the puzzle and how the pieces fit together. They continued:

"All return to the Father and to His love and beauty. All are reborn. This is not the first time you have come to the body, nor shall it be the last. Many of you will come again and again as you have for lo these many years. Some of you remember and understand, though you are not exactly certain how it is so. The souls return continually to the body to test and educate themselves. Man at one time knew this. It is only in your recent history that you have forgotten. The Father's realm is limitless and the learning process so broad that concentration on a specific lesson is extremely difficult. The learning process within the body is more acute, more intense, and more focused, so much so that one is rarely able to learn more than one or two lessons during a lifetime. The conscious mind serves as a barrier to the greater reality known to the subconscious mind. You are only able to see the lesson on which you have chosen to focus for whatever time you will occupy the body. When the lesson has been learned to the soul's satisfaction, you depart, incorporating the knowledge acquired into a larger reservoir of knowledge. Another lesson is chosen and you return with it tucked away within the subconscious, following the same procedure again. Each life varies in that a different body is projected and a scenario more conducive to the particular lesson is chosen. The

souls return to the body until they feel they have obtained sufficient wisdom to reside within the Father's realm permanently
and learn their lessons there. When one becomes enlightened
enough to focus his attention on what is important without help
he will no longer need the assistance of the body to facilitate
understanding. Lessons within the body are rather like looking
through a microscope, using the magnification to enlarge one
particular aspect so that you may examine it more closely. The
body enables one to focus on a particular lesson in all its aspects
and ramifications so that it may better learn wisdom from it. The
body is a school room and the planet Earth is the school house
in which the student resides, nothing more. Life here is nothing
more complex than a learning experience. When your day of
education is done you return home to your Father and loving
family. When the next occasion in which you may learn arises,
you return to the school room to take advantage of the opportunity. This cycle continues until you graduate and return home to
stay. When one has learned all which this particular school has
to offer, he progresses to higher learning within the Father's
world. It is as simple as that, my children. The only complications are those which you insist on adding."

It seemed so clinical, so unromantic somehow. The intensity
of the survival instinct, I suppose, deludes one into placing more
emphasis on the body than was intended. With some deep
thought, however, I did come to understand a great many things
which had defied explanation previously. They elaborated:

"The only way in which a soul may be a part of the Father is
by attaining perfection. In order to attain perfection one must
learn to love perfectly. Eventually, when one has learned all the
lessons he has set for himself, he can begin experiencing oneness
with the Father. Only one has attained perfection, The Christ
who is now one with God. The soul comes eagerly seeking its
lessons, anticipating each one as a step which returns him to the
Father. Upon leaving the body, the soul is aware again of its goal
and begins work immediately, preparing and deciding along
with those of great wisdom what the next lesson shall be. There
are souls who can not recognize their need to learn and continue
to avoid instruction. Some lessons are difficult and take many
lives to learn. Some, unfortunately, are only mastered through

great pain. If a soul slips into the habit of avoiding the more difficult lessons, they accumulate and the intensity with which they must be experienced increases each time the lesson is avoided. When one continually procrastinates, the Father is sometimes forced to place him into a body and an environment in which he will learn."

I did not understand why a soul would avoid what he knew was inevitable or why God did not simply leave them to suffer the consequences of their neglect.

"Discipline is as much a part of love as is affection. The Father must, at times, discipline a soul for its own good in order to protect it from itself. Every opportunity to attain oneness with God is offered. It is only as a last resort that one is forced to assume instruction. Most accept their lessons eagerly and work ardently at accomplishing them. As in all realms, however, there are those who develop a pattern of avoiding their obligations, hoping that there will be an easy way, or that someone will do it for them. Consequently, the Father must force them, like lazy children, to face their responsibilities. Time within the body is brief and when you understand that you have chosen the lessons which you will experience and accept them with grace, then you shall master them quickly."

Why was it so difficult to remember previous existences and lessons learned, I puzzled. It seemed to me that remembering past experiences would make the process go faster. There were, however, many aspects which I had not considered.

"Memory beyond entry into the body is obscured, so that man may focus more intently without being burdened by memories of either past indiscretions, or accomplishments. Memories sometimes cloud one's vision, preventing him from seeing what is in front of him now. You enter each time with a fresh opportunity to make choices, unencumbered by past decisions which were unwise, or overinflated with pride in past accomplishments. You come with a clean slate upon which you may write the lessons of this life. God offers you the opportunity to enter the body repeatedly so that past wrongs or past influences which have lead down the wrong path may be corrected. In this manner one may advance toward oneness.

"The Earth plane is a unique world and the only one of its kind. The inevitable reactions to each action occur quickly within this world. In other worlds the concepts of being are much broader and the reactions not as visible, thus it takes more wisdom to learn and understand the answers when they come. Within the Earth plane you learn quickly that there is a natural order of events and failure to accept and follow that order can result in difficult repercussions. For instance, you learn immediately that if you touch a hot stove your hand will be burned. If you hurt someone, then you must witness their pain. It is a technique which enables the soul to see his lessons played out before him as if he were participating in a play upon a stage."

There is one question, I have found, which inevitably comes up when the subject of coming again to the body is introduced. Why if this hypothesis is true does the Bible make no mention of it? They anticipated this inquiry and explained.

"Your wisdom literature does not speak of coming again to the body because this aspect of the ancient writings was misinterpreted and removed. Man has known of this dictate since he descended into this planet. Some men, however, many years ago within your recorded history, decided to change what had always been a part of the wisdom of the Father. They deliberately obscured knowledge of coming again to the body, fearing it would make man careless about his conduct and behavior. They presumed to possess the wisdom to judge the validity of the ancient doctrine. They saw it as superstitious nonsense created by man as an excuse for not obeying the church and its leaders of that day. The cannon was rewritten with all reference to this subject deleted. Generations since that time have believed the theory to be paganism handed down from an ancient era when man was unenlightened and did not know of the Father and His kingdom. Quite the contrary, those men who took it upon themselves to delete the wisdom of the Father have been responsible for leading generations down the wrong path and for removing what little light was available to man upon this planet from his grasp. An act which will require a great deal of reparation on their part.

"The Father did not scatter His children here like so many seeds to grow wild, be mown down, and thrown into a fire.

Coming again to the body, is a plan devised from the omnipotent wisdom of God. He wishes you to understand that He is a loving Father and would not leave you helpless without a means of rejoining Him. It is no wonder man has trouble believing in the Father's love. The picture conveyed to him is one of a God who cares little for the welfare or plight of those here. This doctrine of returning again to the body is an expression of the Father's deep love for His children."

How, I wondered, if we were children of God was it so easy to trick us into believing false doctrine? They offered:

"Several elements contributed to the deception, among them was your dependency upon others for knowledge, the duplicity of those in positions of power, and the illusions of your plane. Being shut off from memories of past lives, makes one easy prey for those who are obsessed with power and control. You are lost sheep looking for someone to lead you and you often choose the wrong one. You have not taught yourselves to listen to the voice within. Always listen to the Father's voice before you listen to the voice of any man. No man understands the intricacies of His plan as does the Father. No one has the right to tell another how he should respond to the wisdom of God. There is no earthly title which allows one man power over another. Only God has power over all other beings. All earthly beings are the same as you, travelers along a path. God's plan is a problem solving venture which is designed to discover how much ingenuity you can employ and how many problems you can solve, using the tools which you have brought with you. Some do beautifully with amazingly little, others have an abundance of gifts and never accomplish anything. The more one is given, the more is expected. So, do not whine and complain about the difficulties you find along your path. Learn to surmount them or make them disappear. This is, after all, the reason you are here."

I must admit, learning to accept all life's challenges and problems as lessons is often difficult. I have to constantly remind myself to look for the message each event holds. Funny, the little things always seem the hardest. They gently prodded me further:

"Man looks around outside himself and can seem to find no help, or anyone who understands. If he is wise, he turns within.

It is within that you find the Father. Knowing this, will make life within the body much easier.

"The tasks each soul has set for himself may be slightly different, for each is at a different place on the path. Some have more challenging lessons, for they have reached a point at which they wish to test their soul. Something instinctive deep within helps you to realize that you and your brother must help one another. For in helping each other you become stronger and assist one another along the path. The whole point of life is to help each other through the thorns, sharp stones, and difficulties you all face. Love one another. You are all laboring with your lessons and ultimately, you shall all be one.

"The Father wishes you to have this knowledge again because you have been in the darkness far too long. He has waited many years, hoping that you would come to understand that there is another way, another path. You doubt the voice you hear within and can never be certain if your assumptions are correct. You are so easily distracted by the chaos outside yourself. You listen to those reputedly seeking to save you soul. Only the Father can save your soul and only you have the ability to offer it to him. No one holds power over you but the Father. He wishes you to know that the choice is yours and yours alone. If you genuinely wish His instruction and lovingly seek His guidance, you can trust that He will give it. He may not necessarily give you all that you want. He will, however, always give you all that you need. The things you want may not be in your best interest and the Father, knowing this, will give you what is best for you. If you accept what is offered you shall gain the power to control your destiny."

When the sessions had first begun I was so in awe of what was happening and so filled with questions that I had failed to ask one of the most important questions, why me? I am, after all, just an ordinary person, a little more curious than average perhaps, but ordinary all the same. Why were they giving me this knowledge? As usual they seemed to anticipate many of my questions and misgivings before they were voiced.

"The Father wishes you to use the power of love within you to tell your brothers of His divine plan as well as His love and willingness to help them whatever their need. Their views and ideas of God have become distorted by those who use the name of God to wield power."

This gave me pause. I was not sure I was ready to take on the establishment. Confrontation and conflict are simply not my style and I have never had a Joan of Arc complex.

"He will give you all of the support, help and power which is at His command," they soothed. "He will protect you from the wrath of those too narrow-minded to understand. Pay no attention to their threats against you immortal soul, for they have no power over your soul. You come as a messenger from the Father with all His power, love, and beauty to support you, and it is considerable. You need not fear any man, for God is with you, as He is with all those who carry His message. Do not trouble yourself with threats or the unbelief of others. Simply offer His message of love. If it is accepted, then rejoice with your brother that he has found the light and the Father within himself. If the message is rejected, then simply move on, for ultimately each being must find his own way to the truth. You can offer love, beauty, and truth, but you can not force another to accept it. Continue to turn to the Father for assistance, He will guide you and give you strength. He will give you light and wisdom enough to shine from your being so that even a blind man may see."

I kept reminding them that the theory of coming again to the body was one of the most controversial within the Earth plane. They, however, were adamant.

"Life within the body is so limited, How can man possibly believe that one life is enough to attain oneness with the Father? If the creeds of the Earth plane continue in such a limited manner with man refusing to see otherwise, then the belief systems will begin to crumble for they have no basis. Man cries out to the Father, begging to know the truth and when it is sent, he rejects it. Remember the Master's parable of the seeds? The seeds of truth are sown, take root and bear fruit. Other seeds are brushed away or ignored, never bearing fruit. You must recognize the truth when you hear it. With no foundation your beliefs have no hope of survival. They will crumble so that they may be rebuilt again. Many will consider this truth sacrilegious. My children, how if it comes from God, and We assure you that it does, can it be sacrilegious? Do you not understand that nothing in all of infinity has power which is equal to the Father? Why do you fear this concept so? Why do you fear God, a Father who loves you? Why must your God be an angry God who punishes His children? You listen to other men rather than listening to your Father. You listen to the hate and anger and accept it as truth, while doubting the love, benevolence, and wisdom. He is not irritable and impatient with your every flaw. He loves you beyond your capacity to understand. Please, my children, accept His love. It is freely and unconditionally given."

I felt a bit anxious about how this particular portion of the material would be received. They, however, were undaunted and did not understand my reticence. You must understand that to His Wise Ones, truth is truth. They do not understand our evasion of it. They were clearly disappointed with the path the church had taken and would not be put off by my nervousness about how others would feel about what they were saying.

"The Father is deeply saddened by the lack of understanding and compassion among you. He had such high hopes for the concept of the church which came out of the Master's teachings. It was to be a beautiful gathering of ALL God's children. It was to inspire man with the reasons for Christ's entry into the body and an understanding of the necessity of life within the body. He tried to give you the sustenance and courage to accept your lessons with grace and assured you repeatedly that there is no need to fear death. He made attempts to point out all your misconceptions and wrong ideas. Man, however, has again twisted the wisdom of the Father to suit his own purposes. He has changed what he was uncomfortable with, or what he felt gave others an advantage over him. Your present doctrine is not false, it is just that key elements which would facilitate understanding have been deleted. These elements would have helped you to better understand your reasons for being here and your relationship to the Father. You have only portions of what the Master said. You puzzle over them and do not understand, unaware that important aspects have been removed which would clarify His message. Remnants of truth always remain, however, for those who seek them. You are once again being offered the truth. Man comes repeatedly to the body. This concept is a part of God's divine plan to collect all His children into His being once more. The only way you will ever understand the teachings of the Master is to include this concept within them. Stretch you mind, just a little. It is for this reason that your Father gave you free will. Do not allow others to decide for you. If you trust nothing else, trust the Father within you. Seek your answers, my children and do not fear the replies. He will not counsel you falsely."

CHAPTER IX

THE AWAKENING

I must confess, coward that I am, that I considered omitting all the admonitions to the church. I understand that they will not be received favorably and will give non believers plenty of ammunition with which to point an accusing finger. Upon deeper reflection, however, I realized that the whole point of this exercise is to relay the truth and correct past misconceptions. They have given their counsel with the deepest love and concern for the well being of all God's children. I resisted the inclination to alter what was said in order to make things more comfortable for myself. So, with a deep breath and a silent prayer for strength I offer their commentary:

"The awakening, if it can be incorporated into its philosophy, will provide the modern day church with all it has dreamed of. We are afraid, however, that the church will not accept this concept just as the established church of Jesus day would not accept what He taught. Established religions tend to scorn any knowledge which has not been handed down through the annals of church doctrine. Your wisdom literature teaches of the Rapture which is a depiction of the awakening, though most consider this aspect of the teachings rather ambiguous. The awakening (rapture) will be brought about by remembering your true identity and relationship to the Father. As in the Master's day, not all those within the church are narrow minded. Some are openly seeking the truth and will recognize it. Others will do whatever they can to suppress the truth, portraying it as the work of the devil. In the words of the Master, You may know a tree by its fruit. We come bringing the fruit of love. Anger, fear, and hatred are the seeds of bad fruit. How can the devil (if there were such a being) speak of love without defeating the very purpose attributed to him? We bring only love, truth, beauty, and light. They are yours to accept or deny, but blame no one but yourself for your acceptance or denial. Do not create an entity, or devil, who coaxes you away from love. Remember your censure of those who did not believe the Master and your condemnation of their acts against Him? Hold a mirror up to yourself and try to honestly appraise your response to the Father's love. Is it worth the risk that you may once again reject His love, truth, and beauty?

"Essentially, the concept of the Christ which is held by the church is correct, though extremely limited. Little attention is paid to the standard of understanding and love for others which He set for you. He tried to show you by His own example how to live a life filled with love, putting aside the pettiness and mean spirited attitude which carps at your brother's every flaw. He demonstrated by offering love unconditionally, reminding you that as He had, you also would become one with the Father. He displayed, by His own death, that all the Father's children enter His kingdom upon leaving the body. You see Him as a beautiful, benevolent healer and teacher, but you do not allow His messages to penetrate the surface, nor allow them to enter your heart. You must permit His example to affect your life. Love one another as unconditionally as He did. The Master retained understanding of the Father's wisdom when he came. He occupied a body unselfishly and voluntarily to show you that you could also defeat the body and the illusions of your world. He came to show you how to love and to help you to understand that with love anything is possible.

"Man listens far too much to what other men tell him of God and the Christ, not realizing that most other men know little more than he. All men have limited vision and are enclosed within a body which has the same restraints as yours. The Father attempts to speak with you through the messengers He sends who bear knowledge of His love and wisdom. He makes every effort to show you the way to the light. Many laugh and scoff at these concepts calling them the products of superstitious minds. They rejoice as other men tell of the wrath of God, His anger with His children, and His willingness to destroy them if they do not obey Him. You accept this and turn your back on love, believing these expressions of love are from the devil and the wrath and anger are from God. Threats of fear and anger come from men seeking power, not from the Father. If He is a loving God, why would He send His representatives, cautioning of His vengeance and wrath? My children, think with your heart. Anyone who uses fear or anger to bring you to God was not sent by Him. God sends His truth by those who are capable of great love not those who threaten you with reprisal. God does not threaten His children. Do not trouble yourselves with the little power games which use fear and anger to manipulate. They will not survive. They will flail and thrash themselves against the barrier until they are defeated and love shall stand shining and steadfast like a beacon, drawing God's children home. The truth concerning God and the Christ is available anytime you care to listen. The source is within you, as it has been from the beginning of time. You can deny and run from it. You can hide and pretend you do not feel the Father inside you, but He is there and there He will stay. He will love you until you stop thrashing against the stone wall of unbelief and come to Him, allowing Him to love you and heal your wounds."

I suppose that I, like many others, wondered why these misconceptions were allowed to grow and flourish for so long. These doctrines had been formulating for some time. It seemed to me that it would have been easier to nip them in the bud. As usual though, I was thinking with the narrow view of one entrapped within an illusory world. God perceives differently and more expansively with a perfect view of both the future and the past. Despite my childish questions they patiently continued:

"God is destroying all the earthly myths because He wishes His children to know the truth. He is saddened to see you in pain, deluded and sorrowing, begging and crying for help, yet refusing to accept it when it is offered. He wants you to be free to experience your birthright. He wishes to abolish your doctrines of fear, anger, and hatred. They are destructive and hinder your growth. He wishes you to experience the joy and love which being one with Him will bring you. The gift of free will renders God powerless to prevent you from accepting these myths. He again offers you truth and beauty as He has on countless occasions, hoping that you will tire of the power games and of being afraid.

"There is but one God and He is loving, beautiful, kind, and gentle. Incorporated within His being is the only entity to completely accept and be one with that love. There is no room for anything within the Father which does not have its basis in love.

"The present day church is none of the things which God intended it to be. He envisioned a true awakening in which the church would assist all the people of this planet in remembering their connection to the Father and their heritage as His child. One which would allow them to understand that coming into and departing the body is as natural as walking in and out of a door. Had the church responded as He envisioned, there would be little need for coming again to the body any longer. The Father provides all you shall need to learn the truth. He guides you toward it and allows you the freedom to discover it. There is an element of truth in all that you know. You must learn to stretch your mind and expand your vistas to include all that is, eliminating nothing. Even superstition finds its basis in the remnants of a truth which has been carried down from one generation to another, being embellished or deleted by each generation's understanding or lack thereof. Allow the church to provide a beacon of light which will fill all the souls upon your planet, showing them the way back to the Father. The light will soothe their discouragement, calm their fears, and release their anger. Do not continue to be bogged down in dogma and senseless rules which make life there unnecessarily confusing. There is but one rule and that is to love. You must love yourself, love your brothers, and love God. All the rest is just needless complications. Seek to keep love in the forefront of your mind, and all else will fall into place. If the church is to survive, it must nourish love and eliminate fear, anger, and negative thought from its doctrine. Love contains no negativity and no doctrine of sin. The only sin is refusing to love. Learn to love and you shall be free."

A religious doctrine without sin was not going to be easy for the general populace to accept, I mused. After all, guilt and fear of the devil was what kept most people in line. Would not an absence of these deterrents create anarchy within the church? As usual they were ready with an answer.

"The devil which the church sets forth is a composite of all the negative aspects which man has built up down through time.

The devil is not a being, but a collection of negative thoughts and aspects of the human condition. Each time you glorify these elements within your personality, you add to that pool of negativity, allowing it to grow and gain power. Each time you hate, are vengeful, spiteful, or exhibit attitudes which do not find their basis in love you contribute to the power of this pool of negativity. This is what you call a devil. It is the sum total of what you create with your negative attitudes, acts, and refusal to love others. You give the 'devil' power with your indifference and repression of a loving attitude. When you dislike someone, provoke your brother to anger, frighten another, or withhold your love, you convey negative power and allow it to expand. The only thing which has the power to conquer this malignancy is love.

"No one has power over you but God. There is no being who coaxes you into wrong thinking or anger. There is no being who tempts you to be unkind to your brothers. There is no devil waiting to lure you away from God. There is no one but yourself, the Father, and the Master. No other has power over you unless you grant it. The more you allow negative thinking and aspects into your life, the more power you give to them. They can not survive without food and only you can feed them. Overpower the negative aspects of your world with a love which is genuine, gentle, kind, and compassionate. Do not offer others a know-it-all preachy love which threatens him with condemnation if he does not adhere to your beliefs. The church has become a place in which you threaten your brothers with destruction, using the devil as a source of fear to limit another's relationship to the Father. When you do not understand another's means of expressing love, or when it does not agree with your own, you say he is of the devil. My children, no one who can express love, regardless of how meager the expression, is of any devil. A devil is no longer a devil when he learns to give love. Love allows another to depict his own divine spark in his own way. Each of you is unique which delights the Father. Loving your brother does not mean molding him into your image. If you concentrate on love, then all remnants of what you call a devil will simply vanish because you do not give it enough negativity to sustain it.

"Take care the things you give power to. If it is a devil you create, then it is a devil you must face. For what your mind generates, your mind must face within the Nation of the Dead. Let your mind and heart dwell on love. Do not waste your extensive powers or your glorious connection with the Father on anything but love. It is the only thing which is worthy of you."

I must admit that after their dissertation on reaping what you sow, I had totally new ideas about the part the mind plays in nurturing the spirit. It had been easier when there was someone else to blame for the things which were slightly out of sync in my life. Being totally responsible for my attitudes, surroundings, and well being was difficult. No more blaming my parents for my scars and suffering during childhood. No more blaming those around me for the discord and disharmony I found there. I was responsible for my own attitudes and environment. But there is hope they assured me.

"The Father envisioned His church as being a guidepost to ALL mankind, not as a tool with which to threaten His children. The church is to be a place of love, and joy where the Father, Master, and their children may come together, basking in the light and warmth of their shared love. Fear prevents you from accepting His love and seeking His light. The Father stands ready to help you, to provide for your every need and love you for no reason other than the sheer joy of loving you, His beloved child. The Father created love. Man created the devil. Every time you concentrate on love you give power to that love to grow, spread, and encompass all that is near. Each time you respond in love you reduce the pool of negativity which man has built up down through the ages. You are far too beautiful and unique to waste your creative power in negative thinking. Empower all around you by offering the only gift worthy of a child of God ... Love. Love is the strongest, most powerful force in existence. It is the source of the Father's being. It is the love from which the Christ sprang, and it is this same love which begot you, my beloved children. It is your most powerful weapon, your most unique gift, and your most beautiful aspect. You are God's beloved child. If He loves you then surely you can love yourself."

I can never read this part without an overwhelming surge of emotion. I have had a very low sense of self-esteem throughout most of my life. Though I still fight it tooth and nail, I now hold the firm belief that if God believes I can do it then perhaps I can.

As I mentioned earlier, I was raised in the era of "hell fire and damnation" religion. There always seemed to be this battle waging within me about the feasibility of belief in an angry God who was to be feared. They addressed my contemplations.

"Man should not be so afraid of displeasing the Father. This is another of those negative aspects which you have picked up down through the centuries of your culture. The only thing which displeases the Father is your failure to love one another. He is never angry with you. Anger does not exist within His being and He does not wish for it to exist within yours. To fear the Father's anger is to fear needlessly. Anger encroaches upon the space which love occupies, squeezing and choking it out. The Father is incapable of the negative human traits which you attribute to Him. He has no corruption within His being. He and the Master are perfect beings containing only love.

"Make your church a beautiful haven for man, a place in which there are no threats and reprisals, and where one is not weighed down with rigid, unfeeling rules which sap his patience. These aspects create little barriers which enclose each within his own little cubicle, allowing him to only see his brothers narrowly. When love is present, there is no need for rules, restrictions, or distinctions of class, race, language, or religious affiliation. There is no need for distrust, suspicion, or barriers of any kind. There is no need for anyone to be in authority, for all are equal, free, and possessed of their own unique talents. Make your church a place of joy, beauty, and freedom; an open, expansive place where one may come to share love and seek encouragement.

"Your church doctrine is defined by your belief in God and the Christ. The Master came to show you the power of love. He wanted you to understand that He was in command of all the power which the Father possessed. He need not have allowed any of the pain and indignities which were rained upon Him. He did so voluntarily, choosing only to love. He loved those who inflicted the pain and those who shouted insults. He loves even those who seeing all this, still do not believe. With His final breath before departing the body, He asked that the Father love and forgive all of those. He was trying to help you to understand that you have the same power and abilities if you learn to love.

Do not make excuses for not loving your brothers, there are none which are justified. The fact that they do not return your love is totally irrelevant. You are loved and you must love! When you love another there is no desire to inflict harm nor to be angry, or encroach upon him in any way. When your heart is filled with love it will suffice. All of you are equal and share equally in the Father's love. Each of you has an equal portion of the Father's divine being within you. One no more than the other. The reason some seem to have more than others is because they use their gifts more abundantly. Some hide their spark under loud words, accusations, lascivious behavior, and threats of violence, while their divinity cringes in its corner, waiting for all the anger to abate so that the love may blossom. Those who have nourished their spark make it shine forth for all to see. They smile and treat others gently and with kindness. They encourage laughter, joy, and peace. They stand in the light of The Father's love with a smile upon their lips, a glow in their eyes, and kindness and love in their hearts, mirroring the God within. The only way man can find his way out of the twisted maze of beliefs which has been created down through time is across a bridge of love.

"We come offering the Father's gift, wanting only to share our knowledge with you. You can trust that we are sent by the Father because we teach only of gentleness, kindness, and love. Why would you not trust someone who offers you love? What possible harm could these offerings inflict? If love will destroy, then welcome that destruction. If patience will destroy, then by all means allow it to destroy you. If kindness will kill, then you are better off dead. The choice, dear ones, is yours."

CHAPTER X

KARMA

Life's inconsistencies have always peaked my curiosity. The fact that life is often unfair is glaringly evident. How could seemingly innocent children be born hopelessly deformed or into a family situation where they would be cruelly abused and neglected? How were some able to rise above dire circumstances and a less than hospitable environment to greatness, while others were given every advantage only to sink into degradation or ignoble behavior. It is obvious to all that the guilty are not always punished and justice is rarely served. All this supposedly under the auspices of a completely loving, fair, and just God. So, I wondered, what is the leveler? At what point do fairness and justice prevail as we are told they shall? In response to this question they answered with a very detailed discussion on Karma.

"Karma is a means of educating the soul in the proper way to love. The ultimate lesson for the soul is learning to love perfectly and without condition. Since most souls within the body rarely do, it was necessary to create a system whereby one would have guidelines to follow in order to balance himself. Karma is a system of checks and balances set up by the Father so that the soul might keep track of his progress toward oneness.

"Your plane is unique with illusory qualities which make it difficult to discern truth and reality. You can not see others as they really are. It is difficult for most to see beyond the outer shell. The soul which lies within each body is disguised and inhibited to such a degree that He behaves in a manner which is derogatory to his true nature, making it difficult to recognize the reality of his powerful potential. He is insensitive and cruel to others and they reciprocate in kind, neither realizing the grave injustice they do to the being which lies within.

"When the souls descended into the Earth plane, they had not been absent from the Father's kingdom long enough to forget their true identity and natural reality. They could still remember how to return to the source of their being. The longer they remained, however, the more deeply entrenched they became in the maze of illusion. They could no longer find their way back to the Godhead which lay within. Not only could they not find their Father, they could no longer remember where to seek Him. They looked at their brothers and saw replicas of themselves, and realizing that they were lost, they assumed that others must be lost as well. The longer they remained, the more deeply entangled they became until finally they had completely forgotten the concept of real love. The Avatars and the Children of Light, who occupy the higher echelons of the Father's kingdom, volunteered to attempt to rescue the souls from their entrapment. It was apparent almost from the beginning that releasing these souls without their consent or help would be virtually impossible. Attempts had been made to call them back, but they ignored the pleas and plunged in without regard to anything other than their own selfish whims. They disregarded all warnings and no attempt by others within the Father's kingdom could coax them to return. The one irrefutable law set down by God is the law of free will. All God's children are allowed to choose freely without interference from anyone, including God Himself. These foolish children exercised that right. The right of free will was brought to bear for a brief moment, but even this momentary lapse was enough for them to become entangled. Once they were entrapped it was like being in quick sand. They sank deeper and deeper."

As I understood their comments, Man was trapped within the Earth plane because of his own foolish disregard for the preparation needed to enter this plane of illusion. So, had we paid closer attention to the Father's instructions about the preparation needed before entry, we would not be in this mess. Yes, that sounds like me. Impatience has always been one of my major stumbling blocks. They agreed with my assessment and resumed.

"At this point the Father realized that these souls could not, or would not return of their own accord. It would be necessary to create a plan to guide them back toward the path which leads

them to the Father. God in His infinite wisdom decided that the
most beneficial method of handling man's misdeed would be to
allow him to come repeatedly to the body. In the first few
moments of his descent into the Earth plane, man had incurred
many imperfections, tainting his soul to the point that it would
need many lives to return to the perfection with which it had
been created by God. The Children of Light, realizing the trickery of this plane, had, after a momentary descent, returned to the
safety of the Father. They, fearing the plight of those remaining
within the Earth plane, petitioned the Father to be allowed to
guide the others back, assisting them in any way necessary to
ensure their safe return home. The Children of Light, at great
risk to their own being, were allowed by the Father to enter the
Earth plane as a means of assistance to those entangled. The plan
created by the Father to facilitate the rescue of errant souls, had,
up to this point pertained only to matter. It was a system of
action and reaction. A universal law, attesting that for every
action there is a corresponding and equal reaction. The principle
was adjusted to apply to the actions of a soul while within the
body. The record of responsibility for all these thoughts and
actions is called Karma."

I think we have a cliché which seems to bear out this truth. It
says, "What goes around, comes around." They proceeded.

"When one behaves in a manner contrary to his naturally
loving state, then he must learn that such actions are not conducive to the well-being of his soul. He is entrapped in the
depths and darkness of his entanglement unable to see that the
path back to God must be paved with love. Indeed, you often
had difficulty deciding what a loving reaction should be. A
ledger of negative reactions began to accumulate which must be
dealt with. All these unloving reactions and thoughts must be
relearned, regardless of how trivial they seem. In order to be one
with the Father again a soul must be perfect. Within your plane
you associate perfection with behaving in a perfect manner,
never saying or doing the wrong thing, being benevolent, kind,
and piously religious. My children, being perfect does not deal
solely with social behavior, or the physical acts of the body
alone. The body is discarded when it is of no more use to the
soul. Perfection is indicated when a soul has become perfectly

balanced between the positive and negative aspects of being. Positive and negative have nothing whatsoever to do with right and wrong. They pertain to the assertive and receptive aspects within one's being. Positive aspects are assertive, the strong formidable facets which temper a soul, giving it the ability to master its own destiny and stand up for what it knows to be true. The negative aspects are receptive and give the soul its gentleness and sensitivity, its nurturing, tenderness and caring. The object of Karma is to establish the perfect blending of these two aspects within a soul. They only relate to what a soul does physically as it affects his ability to love. When a soul does not, or can not respond lovingly to others then an attempt must be made to correct this insufficiency and imbalance.

"In the Karmic pattern, note is taken that this particular lesson must be worked on. For, if a soul is to be one with the Father again, he must be a perfectly balanced entity. He must be strong and forceful, yet gentle, sensitive, and tenderly loving with others. If one is too strong and assertive, he tends to attempt to overpower his weaker brothers and when carried to extremes it extends toward bullying and cruelty. On the other hand, if a soul is too gentle and sensitive he tends toward weakness and has difficulty knowing when he should be firm and when he should back away. All these traits are incorporated within a loving nature. One need not be weak to be loving, nor a cruel bully to be strong. A loving being is strong and courageous, as well as loving and gentle. Was not the Master so? Was He not tender with the sick and the little ones, yet strong and forceful in the face of injustice? He was firm with those who refused to take responsibility for their own actions. He faced life within your plane and departed unafraid, because He was perfectly balanced and aware that your world was one of illusion. He came to offer you the perfect example of His holy being to follow. An example which would save you from continued entrapment and separation from your Father. Each individual soul must relearn the balance which was lost upon entry into the Earth by taking responsibility for his own thoughts and actions."

I find the fact that my thoughts will be held up to such careful scrutiny terribly disconcerting. Though I am, I suppose what would be considered a reflective person, I realize that a great portion of my thought process is rather undisciplined, not to mention downright catty and unkind. Our world is so concerned with the physical it is very disturbing to think that I will be virtually judged on my thoughts alone. This must be what the Master cautioned us about in the Sermon on the Mount. I can only hope there are points given for good intentions. They proceeded.

"You must remember, my children, thoughts are living things. Once you have a thought it is forever recorded and reverberates throughout infinity. If the thought is loving, then the reverberation is loving. If, however, the thought is on a lower scale of negativity and discord, then the reverberation will be discordant and must be corrected if the soul is ever to enter oneness with the Father again. You must learn as the Master taught, never to judge another by what he does or how he behaves. You can not see the thoughts of another and it is the thoughts and the internal aspects of the soul which survive."

I have been present on many occasions when the Sermon on the Mount has come under discussion. Invariably, when a concrete answer eludes those present, it is agreed that Jesus must have been speaking metaphorically about the importance of anger and one's thoughts. I, however, have never been completely comfortable with this explanation, since Jesus usually said beforehand when the teaching was a parable or allegory. I was not feeling very confident of my ability, both past and present, to discipline my thoughts as they continued.

"Karma is the means by which one corrects the discordant aspects of his being, creating harmony and balance. Karma is a record of all you have ever done, said, thought, felt, or been. It is a golden thread of thought which runs throughout infinity. Impressed upon it is the record of your being and its actions down through time. It is uniquely yours. Each being carries within the pattern of his own karma. If a race of beings acquires an imbalance within its aspect then it is recorded and must be corrected. People who acquire discordant patterns as the result of being a part of a certain group or organization must accept the appropriate karma associated with that group. Along with your own personal karma, you carry intricately woven patterns which concern and affect every soul with whom you have come in contact since your soul's conception. Thus, you can appreciate the intricacy with which each life is planned and patterned so that all may acquire, both collectively and individually exactly what is needed to properly balance their soul."

Once when a friend and I had been discussing the possibility that perhaps we lived more than once, my friend had made the off hand remark that it was too easy. Allowing one to come back and make amends for past indiscretions would promote a complete lack of discipline. Life would become degenerate, amoral, and without purpose. What these wise ones were saying didn't sound all that easy to me. I could after all control what my body did quite easily, controlling what my mind thought, however, was something else again. They continued.

"Your perception of reality is so limited by the illusions of your world that you see little of what lies beyond your tiny cubicle. The patterns of all the souls who occupy infinity are delicately and intricately woven and stretch out to encompass all that is. It is only upon departing the body that one is aware of the relationship of his individual pattern to all the others.

"When man entered the Earth plane he was perfect. The perfect child of a perfect Father. Entry into this plane created a disturbing friction which resulted in discordance and imbalance. The Earth set up illusory barriers which could not be circumvented in the usual way. Suddenly, those who had been accustomed to totally limitless freedom found themselves trapped in a narrow tiny place from which they could not escape. Their response to their condition was something new and unique for them. For the first time, they experienced fear. These beings had never before in their existence been limited and suddenly they found themselves confined within a world they did not understand and which seemed to alter with their feelings about it. They refused to heed the caution of their brothers and found themselves trapped in a mysterious labyrinth from which there seemed to be no way out. Indeed, they began to have difficulty remembering exactly where 'out' was. Fear, the consequence of a lack of understanding, was new to these recently fallen children of God. Fear was the first tainting of those beautiful souls. Their fear, their struggle against a confinement they did not understand, and their inability to release themselves brought about a disastrous consequence, the advent of anger. You see, fear is a natural reaction, but rather than being patient and trying to understand, or accepting help they became angry. They were, after all, they reasoned, the offspring of an omnipotent Father. How dare they be trapped and confined. Like spoiled children, they raged at their inability to release themselves. Now, the most destructive force which can occur within a soul is anger and it tainted these souls immeasurably. Anger is a cancer which spreads, infects and erodes. It creeps into all the tiny crevices of the soul, filling it with darkness and feeding off itself to produce more and more anger.

"The souls had never experienced darkness. They did not understand because their natural home is a place of light. Their Father and brothers are all beings of light. The darkness only compounded the difficulties in which they found themselves. The soul began to look around and see that there were others like himself present. He reasoned that it must be they who were confining him. Regardless of how he implored them, they would not release him, nor would they believe that he possessed the divine right to freedom. His perception was so distorted at this point that he could not see that beyond the facade of the body lay another the same as himself. He blamed his brother for his confinement and the darkness which surrounded him. For the first time in his existence the soul struck out at his brother in anger. This anger set off a chain reaction which reverberated down through infinity and only served to draw him deeper and deeper."

This seemed reminiscent of the Cain and Able story in Genesis, though perhaps even more far reaching than I had realized upon reading it again. They resumed.

"Anger and fear became contagious among the children. They could no longer feel, communicate with, or see the light in themselves or their brothers. The memory of their natural home, their Father and the light filled environment from which they had descended was rapidly fading. It was becoming impossible for them to remember that they were confined at all. Their Father and brothers who were left behind were distressed that the children were striking out at one another in such cruel ways, so completely against their nature. Rescuing these foolish children became of primary concern to all within the Father's world. They no longer heeded the pleas for them to come back, worse still, they were becoming accustomed to their dark little existence and found a perverted sense of security there. As long as they were confined within their little prison with limits which they recognized, they felt secure. They no longer understood freedom and the light which is their natural heritage. Indeed, they were most often frightened of it. When they were approached by a being of beauty and light, they recoiled in fear and shrank from him. They no longer understood love. At this point, it became obvious that no amount of pleading could coax these children from the body and that they were tainted beyond repair. Before they could be welcomed back into the Father, they must in some way be assisted in regaining the true nature of their being.

"Their brothers, all beings of light, asked to be allowed to help and questioned the Father as to how this might be accomplished. The children would not listen and they could not force them. 'How,' they ask of the Father, 'may we help them?' So, God in His divine wisdom decreed that a method of coming repeatedly to the body would be initiated. In this way a soul could enter the Earth plane in a body more suitable to his essence and needs, so that he might relearn all that he had forgotten. He could not remain within the Earth plane indefinitely or he would continue to sink farther into the illusion, making rescue by any means impossible. For this reason, it was felt that the time of their sojourn within this plane should be limited. It was also noted that the bodies which the souls fashioned for themselves deteriorated rapidly within the Earth's environment and the soul continued to deteriorated along with the body if it remained. Thus, the father decreed that in order to stabilize the soul, one must be forced to depart when the body had become detrimental and no longer useful. At such time one would be approached by those within the Father's kingdom and coaxed to return temporarily so that he might be sustained and renewed. At the instant of departure, if he would permit, one would be drawn out by his brothers and accompanied to the Father's world. There he would be apprised of the difficulties incurred, what had been learned, and what was yet to be accomplished. The more severe the instability, the more acute the necessity that it be relearned so that it will not harm the soul beyond repair.

"Certain types of negative karma are approached on a more immediate basis so that they are not allowed to grow beyond the point at which it is impossible for a soul to overcome them. The Father does not wish to burden you unnecessarily or to crush you. Your Father is not now, nor has He ever been, angry with you. He is, however, distressed by the pain which you have brought upon yourselves and the fact that you deny yourselves the freedom, beauty, love, and light which are your natural heritage. God felt that it was important that a soul be allowed to balance the imperfections within himself so that he might readjust his being to fit more comfortably into its rightful place. While within the Father's kingdom, the souls are eager to return and learn their lessons. They are able to view from a more limitless vantage point what lies ahead of them. Realizing how much more quickly deficiencies can be corrected by returning to this plane, they eagerly set about preparing for reentry. The nature of the Earth plane, however, creates very cunning illusions. It wraps itself around you in a warm cloyingly deceptive cloak. Initially, it became apparent that memory of past experiences would be extremely burdensome and the soul became unduly distressed by the memories of past infractions. In light of this, the Father decided that the only effective way to help one deal with the lessons needed was to temporarily obscure his memory. The potential is always there, however, if a soul so desires, to look deeply within and find his connection to the true reality. It takes a great deal of discipline and effort, for this world continually deludes one into believing that any hypothetical reality beyond the confines of the Earth is fantasy. All these elements create a great sense of confusion within the soul. So, the Father in His infinite mercy, obscures your memory. As a soul grows and learns to trust and turn toward the Father for assistance, he may in certain lives be granted pinpoints of memory to expand upon. As a soul attains wisdom within himself, he is allowed to retain that wisdom with each entry if it is felt that it will be of benefit. The wisdom and grace which a soul manages to acquire throughout its sojourns often allows one to rise above much of the pettiness and anger within him.

"Many were sent by God to help these souls to understand their predicament and to remind them of their true heritage. These ministering souls retained more memory and ability because they retreated before being completely tainted by its influence. The entrapped souls viewed these sentinels as supernatural and God-like. Often, they shrank from them in fear, not realizing that the beings brought only love. The beings of light tried desperately to remind the souls of their true identity, lest they forget. They had, however, become so entangled in the greed and darkness of this plane that they began to rely more on one another than those the Father sent. Those corrupted with the lust for power, began attempting to discredit and twist the teachings of the beings of light. As man advanced deeper and deeper into this plane many of the encounters with these beings of light became obscured within their memory and buried in legend. Some faintly remember the joy and beauty of encountering such a being, but with the passage of time man began to overshadow so many memories until the most perfect of all beings asked to be allowed to enter this plane in an attempt to rekindle the spark within mankind. He reminded them of what lay within God's kingdom and that they need only shake off the illusory dust of this plane to attain the true reality. As in all the other occurrences, the wonder and awe that they initially felt from the Master's presence became surrounded and constricted by fear and they began to ridicule Him and sought to cast His presence from them. He departed, leaving behind beings who could carry on the quest for enlightenment. He, too, unfortunately, has become obscured in legend and little of His true purpose is retained in the memory of those who occupy this plane. Many have been sent. Many reside there constantly, disguising themselves as beings much like any other, attempting to gain the confidence of others so that they may assist them in balancing themselves. They seek to guide you away from the destructive aspects of this plane and encourage you to reach toward the Father."

Realizing that nestled within each of us lay a higher self, I wondered why its presence was not more evident, or at least more accessible. They explained.

"Your subconscious is programmed by an extremely enlightened being. It is very powerful and will subliminally direct the conscious mind, feeding pertinent information into it so that one does not become hopelessly lost. It is rare that the conscious mind is strong enough to block the subliminal information."

Could this be what we call conscience, I wondered? Why did the phenomena of conscience seem to be more active in some than others? They continued.

"If one has need of lessons concerning the lower elements then the barrier is stronger between the conscious and subconscious minds, allowing less to filter through. When one has a predestined mission to assist in the betterment of mankind, then the barrier between the two levels of consciousness is very thin, allowing access to much more which can be gleaned anytime it is needed. Often the lack of access to one's subconscious is a tool employed to teach him to reach beyond himself for assistance.

"Coming and going in and out of the body is the whole essence of your existence within the Earth plane and the sole purpose in your being here. It is no great mystery, nor is it excessively complicated. The Father does not allow His children to come into the body casually. Coming and going in and out of the body is no more a game than karma is a mere score sheet. It is a divine plan initiated by a loving omnipotent Father. A plan in which His children may reeducate themselves and return to their once radiant glory. When a soul enters the body, the teaching tools are incorporated into the body assumed by the soul. We ask that you accept for the purposes of clarification, the allegory that the Earth is a school room. You were conceived from the being of a loving Father, cared for, and nurtured as the precious child you are. At some point you began to venture out on your own, testing your own capabilities. The Father realized that certain elements of your being and creative abilities were not adequately prepared to deal with the kind of illusions present within the Earth plane. He decided that you should be properly prepared so that you might attain your fullest potential. Now, just as there are different schools on different levels of education within your plane, so it is within the Father's world. The Earth is one level of school. There are other worlds which have other levels of learning for the soul, but the highest level of instruction occurs within the Father's kingdom. When one enters His kingdom all barriers disappear and one is privy to all knowledge and may avail himself of any guidance that he is capable of understanding and absorbing. The Father designates certain beings within His kingdom to assist in the preparation of each soul before they enter their respective worlds to begin their education. All the physical attributes, or the lack there of, incorporated within the body serve as instruments of education. The level of one's intellect and ability to absorb knowledge is a tool, as well. There is also intuitive and instinctive awareness which has nothing to do with intellect and can be very valuable to a soul. Often, within your plane, you dismiss a lack of intellect, unable to understand how helpful and creative one with strong intuitive powers can be. Both are valuable. One can be taught, the other is inherent. One has to do with intelligence, the other with wisdom. Do not sell one short who is intuitive and possessed of a sympathetic attuning to his environment and the other creatures who populate it. A soul is never encouraged to concentrate on one aspect to the exclusion of the others, regardless of how gifted he may be. The object is balance, perfect balance. The only way in which an imbalance can be corrected is in your acceptance that it exists. When you have learned to accept with grace and rise above the imbalances within your being, then they will, perhaps within the next sojourn, begin to abate and disappear. It is like the weight scales with the tiny trays on either side. If one tray is overloaded the other must be balanced or the soul will plummet downward into destruction. It matters not how good and positive you consider a pursuit, obsession toward one aspect, to the exclusion of all others, is destructive.

"All the situations and circumstances in which you find your-self are of your own making and design. It is important that you understand this. However difficult one's circumstances may seem, they do not occur at the hand of anyone other than them-selves for the express purpose of balancing their soul. This is an important lesson which you must learn, for when you under-stand then you can deal with these situations, or help another to deal with them. Allow others to acquire the experience necessary to deal with their own life styles, attitudes and abilities, or the lack there of, gracefully. These are the things which will create or destroy the balance of the soul. We do not mean to imply in any way that you should not offer others comfort, love, compassion, encouragement, or assistance when you are able to do so. You must remember, however, that you can not learn another's lessons for him and in attempting to do so you do him a great disservice. It is more beneficial if you assist one in accepting what he has chosen with grace, changing his attitudes so that he may learn and rise above it. Thus, a soul will gain much needed balance and strength."

That seemed simple enough, I thought. Right! All I have to do is change my attitude about something and it will change to suit my feelings about it. Any of you who have ever wrestled with a habit you wanted to break realize that this is, contrary to public opinion, no simple matter. Changing the way you feel about something, particularly something which irritates or makes you angry, can be even more difficult than a physical addiction. It is so easy to hide your feelings inside and pretend that all has been forgiven and forgotten. When you do this, as I quickly found out, you are fooling no one but yourself. They elaborated.

"When one strains against and resents his lessons, allowing himself to become angry and bitter about the events which occur in his life, he only intensifies the difficulties. You blame God for punishing you and pile up even more negative attitudes which must be adjusted at a later time. You must understand that everything you think, feel, say, or do throughout your soul's entire existence is indelibly impressed upon a skein of memory which runs through infinity. This skein of memory is called the Akashic Record. All the souls which exist, their comings and goings, their actions, feelings and utterances whether harmonious or discordant are recorded permanently upon this skein of memory. You can not alter what you have done, thought, said, or felt, but you may build upon it. You can use past events and attitudes as a reference or turning point. You can accept with grace and love yourself as you are, using all the resources available to you as a means of rising to new heights. You can use these resources to elevate the imprints left by your thought patterns, encounters, and the affect of your presence on the events which surround you. You must understand that these events, attitudes, and thoughts are the building blocks and foundation upon which your existence throughout infinity is built. They affect not only you, but all those whom you encounter and with whom you interact. It is important that you learn to balance your attitudes, being neither too emotional, nor devoid of

feeling. Neither is a good balance. Learn to accept what is right-
fully yours to learn and change, dealing gracefully with the ramifications and reactions of your soul in previous times. You are
never asked to pay another's debts, nor learn another's lessons.
You are only held accountable for your own actions. You must
accept the ramifications of any force you bring to bear upon the
life of another which distorts or alters their natural course and
inclinations. You must pay scrupulous attention to the influence
you have upon others, particularly the young ones, or those who
are less aware. While it is true that all events are intertwined and
carry a karmic lesson, your influence upon another can serve to
encourage or discourage, to inspire or to crush. If you crush
another, regardless of the provocation, you are responsible for
your part in any impairment incurred. Do you see the importance of loving responses, both for you and for others? We do
not mean to imply that you should not interact with others, but
it is important that you do so lovingly. You can break a negative
karmic cycle with another simply by refusing to respond in any
fashion other than lovingly. The actions of another, or their
provocations matter not at all, other than as far as they affect
your response to them. If you refuse to respond in anger and
choose instead the loving rejoinder, then the cycle of negative
reaction with that particular individual may be broken. You are
not responsible for the reactions of the other being involved,
only your own. The whole purpose of entry into the body, after
all, is to learn to interact lovingly with others, something which
was inherent within your nature before entry into this world.
Transform your attitudes concerning others and your circumstances, by accepting your responsibilities. Even the most difficult lessons, when accepted gracefully, can be made easier."

Looking back over events of my life, I could see that this was
true. When I had strained and fought, things only seemed to get
more tangled. When my daughter died, I raged in anger at the
circumstances and found nothing but pain and darkness. It took
a lot of searching to find the light again. The search, however,
culminated in the loss of another child which was accepted more
gracefully, if no less painfully. My refusal to taint his memory
with anger allowed me to establish a connection with another
reality and join Shane and those who occupy that realm, in the

joy of sharing the wisdom I found there with those of you who are here. They concurred.

"The beauty and light of a loving attitude attracts legions of those within our world who are eager to help. Your lessons are only compounded by anger and bitterness and the darkness of this kind of attitude, drawing you deeper into entanglement. Remember, the object is balance. Your life will be equal amounts of pleasure and pain. The grace with which you accept your lessons and the diligence with which you work at them will determine the difficulty and manner of the lessons in the future."

I learned very quickly that just because I understood the process did not mean that I could relax and forget about having to work at learning. The euphoria of knowledge soon abated and returned to the drudgery of the everyday struggle toward balance. They continued.

"One is never given more than he is capable of learning, nor more than he has the ability to surmount. The Father has no wish to crush, or burden you unnecessarily. This would be counter-productive and completely nullify the success of His plan. The Father's intention is to draw His children back into oneness, not send them down to despair and destruction. The despair one feels is often brought about by one's own anger, bitterness, and refusal to accept one's irresponsible attitudes. Relinquish your anger, accept responsibility for your own actions with the grace of a true child of God. This is not meant to imply that one who accepts with grace shall have no more lessons to learn, nor the need to seek an upward trend in their evolution. One may not simply lie down and say do with me as you will. An entity must actively participate in his evolution; otherwise, there can be no growth. Accept your lessons, understanding that they are yours and vowing that you will complete them with as much grace and positive thinking as you are able. Ask the assistance of the Father and those within His kingdom. They will help you to find the strength and resources needed to accomplish the goal you have set for yourself. When this is done, then you will proceed to the next set of lessons until you climb the ladder upward into the light of oneness with the Father. Amen!

"If you are incarnate within the body, then you are at some point on the evolutionary spiral that is a part of becoming one with the Father. It is difficult at times to explain to you the process by which a soul travels ever upward, for this process does not always seem to be so within your plane. There are some who seem to be digressing rather than progressing. There are those who seem to display a great degree of animosity and negativity toward others without ever paying the price for such behavior. What you do not realize is that the affect is cumulative. Over a series of lifetimes one can accumulate quite a storehouse of negative, discordant attitudes, making no attempt to alter or modify their insensitivity in any way. If one continues to ignore his own reckless irresponsible behavior, then often the price will be required of him all at once. The bill always comes due. Always! There seem to be a great many injustices and imbalances within your world if you do not understand the karmic learning process. You see, many, because of their lack of initiative toward responsibility must choose lives which seem to be very harsh and cruel so that they might better learn to appreciate the responsibility which accompanies their true nature. So, when you encounter those who seem to be unjustly afflicted either physically, mentally, or by the cruel circumstances of their lives, do not accuse God of smiting them with His wrath. Try and understand that one only assumes the consequences of his own past actions and unloving behavior. It is not inflicted upon him unjustly by a vengeful, angry God, but rather he is allowed by a loving Father one last chance to fulfill his anticipated potential as the loving creature he was meant to be."

During these sessions I always took the opportunity, like any mother, to check on Shane's progress. He had mentioned that he was with the aide of wise counselors, going through a review of His life. I was very interested in the process and what they were appraising. He replied that they were examining events carefully one at a time. They were at that particular stage examining his childhood, to see how loving he had been. I told him to tell them that I said he had been a sweet little boy. He thanked me warmly and replied that this was evident when and if present. They explained:

"Between sojourns within the body, the soul is allowed a panoramic view of his existence. He is encouraged to weigh the positive and negative aspects and the degree of balance between the two. He is counseled by those wiser than himself about what may be done to affect a more perfect balance. When one is within the Father's kingdom his view of reality is unobstructed and he is able to see his goal with more clarity. Oneness with God becomes the single motivation for existence. No sacrifice is too great to attain that goal. One is counseled in the reasons for the present imbalances and the manner in which they may be amended. It is rarely possible for one to attain the necessary balance within a single lifetime. Upon entering the Father's world between sojourns one is able to recognize that he can only make small strides upward on the spiral in one lifetime. The pace is slow, but it is ever upward. One weighs the imbalances and matches them to the proper quotients for correcting them, chooses the necessary tools, and enters the body. It is virtually impossible for one to avoid accumulating some added negativity, but every effort is made to keep it minimal.

"As the soul begins to steadily mount the spiral of evolution, the veil between his conscious mind and super conscious mind grows thinner. He responds more readily and in a more congenial fashion to the subliminal messages from his subconscious. Evolution would be accurately depicted as a spiral which is one continuously evolving circle traveling ever upward as each circumference grows progressively smaller. On each of these spirals is an infinite number of souls, each working diligently to advance one painstaking step at a time upward toward the Father. The graceful learning of one's lessons and love propels him upward. A soul and his counselors take great care to choose the lessons which will lift it a little each time. Regardless of how small the step, one must progress upward. When a soul acquires a particularly large amount of anger and negativity within one lifetime and it is feared that his progress will be seriously impeded within future sojourns, then he is held in a state which allows him to regain his strength and sense of direction. This state is temporarily devoid of awareness. In this manner he will not digress, incurring insurmountable karma. These souls are nurtured and cared for until they are able to resume. There are individuals who acquire negative karma far beyond their ability to repay, and indeed, show no desire to, regardless of the patience and love with which they are counseled to do so. In such instances the Father has no alternative, the only merciful thing which can be done is to obliterate the soul. This is neither done casually for minor infractions, nor until every possible avenue and incentive has been attempted and examined. Repeated efforts are made to encourage the soul to attempt even the smallest step toward recompense. However, when repeated attempts have been made to no avail, there is no other alternative. A soul must actively participate in his own evolution. This is a sad event, one which affects us all. Many of the things which you are led to believe within your plane bring about such an event, do not. It is rarely the result of a single infraction, but rather a collection of continued, repeated refusals to take responsibility for one's actions. Often, within your world there are certain social taboos which you feel most certainly damn a soul, but this is not the case. There are many times when negative aspects are needed to balance or teach a soul understanding for the weaknesses of others. These may be the tools for teaching compassion and understanding. When a soul leans too far toward the positive side, making it rigid, then negative aspects are often introduced to promote balance and understanding."

This aspect of the teachings was difficult for me to grasp at first. We are taught so specifically that there is good and bad. I was forced to take another look at a Father whom I had always condemned as bad because of his alcoholism. I was beginning to see that perhaps my assessment of others with the limited tools I possessed might be somewhat faulty. They were patient but they agreed.

"It is for this reason you are cautioned against judging your brothers. You are not equipped to judge another, for you can not possibly know what is needed to balance their soul. This can only be done within the Father's kingdom where the perspective and wisdom is limitless. So, take care not to condemn others too harshly for what you see as negative traits. You can not possibly know the pattern of their soul and what is the best path for them. Only the wise counselors who reside within God's world know and they answer only to the Father Himself. Instead, concentrate on attempting to balance your soul, which is, in itself work enough. If each individual were to concentrate on the love needed to bring about balance within his own soul, then he would have little time to decide what his brother should or should not do. Respect another's right to attend his own soul without your judgmental interference. Learning this exalted lesson will acquire for you another step on the upward spiral. Contemplate and meditate on the concept of the spiral. Take care that you are not too satisfied with what has been accomplished, nor too discouraged by what has not. All shall transpire in its own time. You must continually seek the Father. You have only begun and must work diligently to propel yourselves upward. The propulsion is activated by a loving heart which seeks only what is best for another and what will lift him toward the Father. Do not attempt to cast another in a mold of yourself. Allow him the freedom to find his own means of progression without any condemnation from you. Contemplate these concepts deeply, for they are the most loving lessons which can be offered to another. Before offering them to another, however, one must learn them within himself.

"When one begins his ascent of the evolutionary spiral there are certain cyclic events which are brought about by his quest. As a soul matures, so, in like manner do his lessons. While they are perhaps the same lesson, one may experience a more mature version. It is for this reason that in your plane history appears to repeat itself. One approaches his lessons on a level which befits his stage of growth. As his comprehension matures he advances to the next phase or degree of understanding. The lessons are very broad in their concepts. They are incorporated within a series of events brought about on a level associated with your potential. They teach love, patience, understanding, and compassion. These are not things one can learn in a single lesson or sojourn within the body. One learns to reflect these attitudes in all aspects of his being gradually over a long period of time. He begins as an infant who must learn to crawl before he can walk. So, one must learn the elementary rudiments of love, patience, understanding, and compassion before he can learn the more mature aspects of the unconditional expressions of these attributes. The lessons are introduced in categories which bring about this learning and evolution. It is a natural progression from learning to love and individual close to you to unconditionally loving all other beings. The affect is cyclic as one begins at a point on a circle, progressing from one stage of development to another until he has accomplished all the lessons laid out on the entire circumference of the circle. When one approaches the end of the lessons available on the circle and approaches the point at which the end and the beginning converge, the circle lifts upward with another slightly higher circle. Each ascending circle repeats the process on a higher level, thus the spiral effect. The object of these repeated cycles is the necessity that a soul learn to love without thought of self and to be patient, regardless of the price. With patience and love come an inward sense of serenity and knowing that whatever the obstacles along the path, you can surmount them, retaining your strength and sense of purpose. You must relearn the rudiments of love and patience, an awareness you sacrificed with your hasty unprepared descent into this plane. You must rid yourself of the terrible stigma of anger which has brought such destruction upon your soul. Free yourselves of the shame and replace it with love. It is a long and arduous task, but if one could accomplish such a task by simply being told that he must, then the souls would not have become entrapped in the first place. When it became apparent that the illusions of your plane interfered with the communication necessary for a soul to understand the higher aspects of being, it was imperative that another method of learning be established. The lessons must be learned by rote and practiced over and over until they become an instinctive part of your mental process. When the soul reaches the point at which the lessons become almost involuntary, the veil between the conscious and subconscious mind becomes thin and they are able to avail themselves of the higher wisdom which is available. As one learns to accept the directives of the higher mind rather than the lower elements of his nature, then he is said to be enlightened. When one reaches this point in his evolution it is not necessary to continually prompt him to display love and kindness toward another. He begins to radiate light, a light which has been shrouded in darkness by the negativity acquired from occupancy within that plane. Negativity, anger, and the lower elements of being tend to create a dark, dismal clouding of the soul. When one rises above these lower elements and responds to the higher more spiritual aspects of being, then the light begins to spread outward from his core, emanating a shining radiance which is visible to all."

I had always imagined that all enlightened beings only resided within the Father's world and was pleased to find that this was not the case. I had also assumed that you must be on a level with the Christ to be classified as enlightened. This also was a misconception. I thought back to the time when I had seen Shane, his face and being radiant with light, depicting a beauty far beyond any earthly manifestation. I asked if this was a reflection of enlightenment. They replied that it was.

"When one attains this degree of enlightenment his inclination is to show others the light, ridding them of their darkness and fear. One believes if he can but allow others to see the light they will recognize its significance and seek to possess it themselves. In his eagerness, he is saddened that others are frequently suspicious of his motives and fail to detect the importance of the light. One of the lessons which a newly enlightened soul must learn is that each must find the light for himself. One must of his own accord banish the darkness and seek the light, for it exists in great abundance all around him. Each must find his own truth and light. It is not within your power to instill the light within another. You may teach others where it lies, encourage their quest, and support them when they falter, but each must find his own way. Each has his own path and must make the climb himself. He can not hold onto another's coat tails and ride effortlessly upward without exerting any effort himself. If one needs assistance, then he must humble himself to ask for it. This is the reason he presently occupies the body and experiences the cycles of learning which repeat themselves over and over.

"There is only one set of lessons which continually evolve upward on the spiral. As a soul approaches the advent of a new circle, it is generally heralded by a climactic event which pushes one upward toward the new circle. He must leave the old behind and mount the new higher path which leads him toward love, patience, and understanding. The bricks which pave these paths and lead toward oneness are the lessons which one experiences in his sojourns within the body. Your soul records the lessons, accumulating them down through aeons of time. When one is attentive he may be aware of certain knowledge which filters from the storehouse of the subconscious into his conscious awareness, dictating his responses to others. When you allow the higher aspects of your being to impose your responses, then your soul begins to lift upward. Your true nature as a child of God lies within your subconscious mind incorporated within the memory of all you have been down through time. When you reach enlightenment and the barrier between your conscious mind and your higher self thins, you may probe the subconscious, living by its dictates and using them to overcome the obstacles which lie in your path. When one can accomplish this he has truly become the spiritual being he was intended to be and will be better able to respond to others with patience. You must learn how to reach the wisdom inherent within you and follow the path upon which it leads you, for each is different and conforms to the lessons which produced it. When one has learned to trust the wisdom of the Father and the love it generates, then he seeks the higher wisdom and gradually learns to respond more and more to the knowing which lies deep within his soul. His progress becomes more constant as the circles narrow and he begins to steadily mount the upward spiral of evolution. There lies but one mastery at the summit of the spiral, a loving oneness with your Father and brothers."

I can remember once, remarking to Shane that I had decided if I only learned one thing in this lifetime, I was going to learn to be patient. He replied by draping his arm around my shoulder and commenting, "Mom, if raising me has not taught you patience, you can't be taught." Perhaps. Nonetheless, I think they often sensed when I was groping for understanding and bewildered by the effort. In such instances they would attempt to explain more thoroughly.

"We would like, if we may, to use another allegory to illustrate the cyclic progression of the lessons which face man. We suggest that you imagine a spiral progressing upward in ever narrowing circles, converging on a single point at the top. We would ask you, for the sake of clarification, to imagine that the circles are formed with a series of blocks. Each block contains its own lessons and challenges to be learned. Each soul stands on a particular block and is only allowed to concentrate on the things which enhance his knowledge and experience of the lesson contained within his block or space. All the blocks which form the circle contain lessons which teach love, patience, understanding, compassion, kindness, and all the infinite variables contained within these qualities. For instance, if you are standing on a block which teaches patience, then you will be given or draw to yourself lessons which expand on and increase your ability to be patient. The lessons can be very broad, depending on what is needed in your case. The variables are endless, but all are designed to increase your ability to concentrate on and increase your level of patience. When you have learned the full extent of the lessons contained in that space, then you may move on to the next which may deal with lessons in love. You will occupy all the blocks for a time until you have learned what each has to teach, progressing upward until the lessons are fine tuned. One learns the consequences which occur when he fails to be patient with the failings of another, or the harsh lessons which come from the bitterness which causes him to withhold love. One learns to forgive, and to love unconditionally, without expecting love in return. You learn to be patient with another's inability to love or to appreciate love when it is offered. As the circles narrow and lift upward toward the light, the lessons are fewer and become more difficult. However, one's understanding and ability to accept his lessons with grace increases, so, one balances the other. When one reaches the point at which enlightenment is conveyed, then he understands that help is available and uses all his resources more wisely. Each soul travels on a spiral which is uniquely his own, yet blends with those of his brothers. It is a paradox, containing the wisdom which declares that all are unique, yet all are one. Understanding this premise will increase your knowledge immeasurably. Each soul vibrates to its own unique pattern and bears the stamp of his own wisdom and knowledge upon that pattern for all infinity. When the evolution of all the souls is complete, then there shall be only one. Within this paradox lies the wisdom of the ages. We understand that often life within your plane is difficult, particularly when dealing with others who do not understand what lies beyond the material plane. It is our wish to give you patience, love, courage, and to remind you that no obstacle is insurmountable, be it human or otherwise."

CHAPTER XI

ALL GOD'S CHILDREN

I felt old, established ideas begin to melt away, creating a sense of fluidity which conformed to no set mold, but flowed easily over new concepts. I wanted to know more about those who reside within the Father's kingdom.

How were they different from we who are here within the Earth plane. Like a child I wanted to know, do they eat, sleep, laugh, work, play. Exactly what does one do to occupy himself for all infinity. I was to discover they were often a bit perplexed by my sense of humor. However, they tolerantly endeavored to provide whatever I wanted to know, as long as it did not interfere with a future choice to be made either by myself or someone of my acquaintance.

"All God's children were created at once. Not all who occupy the Father's kingdom were created the same, however, for the beings found there are many and diverse. There are the ranks of angels, cherubim, seraphim, and archangels to name a few of the more familiar ones. There are wise ones, elders, and Avatars. These are each unique unto themselves, both as groups and as individuals. The children, as all other beings, were created simultaneously by a loving thought of the Father. The Father wished for all the worlds throughout infinity to have the advantage of His love. It was His desire, in that divine loving thought from which His children sprang, that they convey the love which was within Him throughout all creation. He intended to prepare them for entry into their respective worlds, instructing them in the intricacies and uniqueness of each world, as well as, the idiosyncrasies and illusions of each. Every world has its own particular level and can be used to its best advantage by souls who are well prepared to use its attributes wisely. Most of the souls entering the other worlds prepared themselves adequately,

129

but the Earth plane was different. The souls were intrigued by what they saw there. It possessed a strange allure which some of the others did not have, an intriguing little game which all felt equipped to play and were certain they could win. They did not see the need to wait for preparation and entering without the needed adaptation, they became hopelessly entangled. Thus, creating a mystery which has absorbed man for aeons. You were all created simultaneously and equally bestowed with the gift of the Father's divine love and potential. It is your use of your gifts which makes it seem as though you are a victim of inequality.

"Some beings are closer to the Father than others. There are those who have access to more information and have closer communion with Him. Communion with God is not something one can do from any level. One can petition or speak to Him and recognize the Father within himself. But, to actually commune with the Father, to mingle with His essence and draw from it the wisdom, light, and love, transmuting and communicating it to others is something only a select few are able to do. This exceptional ability must be acquired over countless aeons of time. One must work diligently to prepare himself, to make himself loving and patient enough to quiet his being and accept within himself the light of God. The Avatars are closest to the Father, for they are more near to perfection than most. They do not descend into the flesh other than by choice. They have retained within their being the level of perfection and aspect of the Father with which they were created, producing a being more exceptional than all others. The Wise Ones and Elders were gleaned from the souls which populate the Father's worlds. They are souls who have attained the highest degree of enlightenment and wisdom. A level which is very near to that of the Avatars. They are the purveyors of wisdom and knowledge. It is they whom others of God's kingdom consult when in need of wisdom and counsel. None are wiser, save the Avatars, the Father, and the Christ. The Christ, who was an Avatar, is the only being who has attained perfection and rejoined Him.

"The angels and the angelic kingdom are unique unto themselves. They do not evolve as the souls do. They are always what they were created to be, the Father's messengers. They carry out their holy office, transmitting God's words and messages to His other children. They are beings of service and obtain sustenance and joy through serving others, whether they be within the Father's kingdom or without. It is these three groups of beings who are closest to the Father. They retained their closeness because they did not descend into the flesh. These beings were wiser from the beginning. However, being able to commune with the Father more easily does not mean that they are loved more than His other children. All are beloved of God and He has no wish that any should perish. All are loved and have the opportunity to raise themselves level by level, dimension by dimension through this world or any other toward oneness with Him. This is the message which we bring you."

It was very hard to grasp with my finite mind that some were not more exalted than others within God's kingdom. I felt, even in my encounters within the dream state, very much in awe of these glorious beings. It was hard to understand them stooping gently to help such a thick headed child as myself. Being within the body made some of the loftier concepts seem like fantasy. It was easy to see why man had been so easily duped. They were, however, both patient and adamant.

"Some within the Father's world are wiser than others because they have worked diligently at their lessons. Others were wiser from the beginning. There are those to whom the Father has entrusted the wisdom within His being. They bear the responsibility of conveying that wisdom to all His other children. It is these Wise Ones whom we consult before communicating this knowledge. The Avatars are wiser still. Their likeness and essence is so near to that of the Father that man within the Earth plane would have difficulty discerning the difference between an Avatar and God. The Avatars possess traits and characteristics which are unique within the Father's kingdom. The Wise Ones and Elders specialize in wisdom, the law, and knowledge of the law. We do not speak of rules and regulations, but of universal law. There are certain laws which the Father has set down to bring order to all infinity and the beings who occupy it. This is referred to as Universal Law. The Wise Ones and Elders are privy to the knowledge and wisdom which governs all worlds and life. They are privy to the Akashic record; are, in fact, the keepers of those records, and possess the greatest wisdom in translating their contents. The Wise Ones and Elders do not enter other worlds or leave the Father's kingdom. It is only within the Father's world that there is sufficient limitlessness to contain the potential and probabilities which make that wisdom and knowledge feasible.

"The Avatars, unlike the Wise Ones and Elders, can enter other worlds and do so on occasion. They are beings of service and love who enter a world in order to assist man and guide him along a higher path, indeed, they show him the path and the correct way to traverse it. They have unique and diverse abilities which no other beings possess. They are able to create with a thought anything which is needed to assist them in their mission. They are able to affect others with their thoughts and create illusions which will serve their purposes and needs at the time. They have the ability to reach into a beings mind and affect the knowledge contained there. They fill it with light, making all knowledge easier to understand. Avatars are able to completely circumvent the illusions and trickery of the Earth plane without being influenced by them. These two groups are wiser than any within the Father's kingdom. Each level and dimension has its masters who preside over and assist the souls who abide therein in whatever manner they are able. Those who supervise each level and dimension are able to consult with those within the higher echelons of the Father's world. They may consult the Christ, the Elders, and the Avatars whenever the need arises. All masters have attained a degree of enlightenment which is far above the souls within their charge."

The term *Avatar* was new to me. I had never been aware of their existence before now and wanted to know more about them. They complied.

"An Avatar's wisdom is obtained directly from the Father who is the seat of all wisdom, knowledge, beauty, and love. It is only they who are perfect and loving enough to remain within His holy presence. They were not so foolish as to stray from God. This truth was told by the Master in the parable of the prodigal son. These stayed with the Father, basking in the light of His being, and absorbing into theirs the light, love, and wisdom contained within Him. The other souls, like the prodigal, went in search of adventure. Though they were warned that not all things are as they seem to be, like foolish children, they refused to heed the warning and became entrapped. They will be welcomed home with love and celebration as the true children of the Father, sharing equally with their brothers who did not venture from their Father's side. The wisdom obtained by the Avatars, the Wise Ones, and the Elders is contained within the light which is the mind of God. The light permeates their entire being and illuminates them with love, wisdom, and beauty. All God's children are privy to the light, but only a small portion realize their potential and take advantage of the privilege. Only a very few are able to absorb all of the light into their being, translating its wisdom so the rest may understand. All knowledge comes from the Father. There is no other source nor any other who has the wisdom and authority to understand all that is. Many have been in the darkness for so long that accepting the Father's light fully into their being is not possible. When one has been in the shadows for so long he must become accustomed to the light gradually or else he will be blinded and unable to see. This is another way of expressing the term evolution. When one evolves he gradually, one step at a time, becomes accustomed to the light. With each step you are able to absorb a little more until you have climbed all the stairs and are able to open yourself fully, accepting all the Father's light. This has been your destiny from conception. When you are able to accept God's light, then you like your brothers who are Wise Ones, Elders, and Avatars, will be privy to all that is contained within that light. The path to wisdom, dear ones, begins with a single step. Each step taken upward enlightens your being more. We are here to encourage your faltering steps so that you might illuminate you being and come one step closer to the Father. When you are one step closer, then all are one step closer. Until we all enter, then none of us may enter. You see, dear ones, not only are we responsible for our own evolution, but for that of our brothers as well. We climb the ladder together.

"When you can open your being to the light, allowing it to enlighten you and enabling you to commune directly with the very source of your being, then you no longer need the step by step path to evolution within the body. At this point in your growth His light can simply draw you up. When you have learned to recognize the Father and His light, realizing that He is the source of your being, then you may be nurtured by the

Father directly without the need for steps, levels, and dimensions. When one can open himself enough to see the Father within and His reflection in others, then he will realize that whatever form the outer shell takes all beings are the same. Open yourselves. Allow the spark of God within you to be fanned into a glorious flame, converging with all other flames into one beam of light. Reach into the stillness of your being and find the spark. It resides within your soul.

"Within the Father's kingdom evolution never becomes automatic. The need to learn and grow is constant until a soul has perfected itself. With the cessation of growth one stands still and stagnates, regardless of the level or dimension on which he exists. You can never stop reaching upward toward development. Until all are one and have evolved into perfection, then none are completely free and at rest within the Father. Each of you evolves individually and uniquely within his own being while evolving collectively with all his brothers. You must aid and assist another in his growth when it is possible for you to do so. No matter what your level, the dimension you attain, or the wisdom within you, until you are one with God, then your growth is not complete and must be sought above all else. Only the Christ is perfect. He attained this exalted state by voluntarily entering the Earth plane which is by far the most difficult of the evolutionary planes. He overcame the difficulties within that world, while remaining untainted by it. He prevailed in His loving attitude and never lost sight of His heritage, His true home, and His Father. He agreed to descend as the humblest of men with few material possessions to prove to man that material things are of little consequence within the grand scheme of things. He came armed only with the love, beauty, and wisdom which lay within His divine manhood. He came to show all other travelers on the path that there was a means by which they could be released. Because He chose to walk this path as other men do, remaining pure, loving, and untainted by its illusions, He attained perfection and oneness with the Father. He endured harshness, cruelty, and rejection that few men within your plane experience, yet never allowed it to deter Him. His vision remained true, without obstructing His purpose. He always remembered that He was God's child, and as such, was a completely loving and divine being. He serves as a glorious example to us all. Amen.

"Your guides and teachers within the Father's kingdom are those who have attained levels of evolution which lie beyond yours. Each level and dimension has its teachers and those who help the others who are in their charge. There are countless levels within a single dimension and many divisions and groups within a level. Explaining the limitless spectrum which lies within each, is virtually impossible. There are twelve dimensions and they are of immeasurable proportions. Many have attained levels of perfection within a dimension and have evolved to a point at which they can offer their brothers the benefit of their experience. It is extremely important that a soul not be burdened beyond his abilities. We strive to see that no soul is overwhelmed to the point of discouragement. It is extremely important to all of us here that each soul reach his fullest potential and experience the triumph which comes through overcoming obstacles laid down by the self. It brings us great joy when a soul understands why a stumbling block is there and accepts the lesson with grace. All of us here celebrate your victories along with you."

I remembered when I was a child and had, I am sure, driven my mother to distraction with my ceaseless questions about why things were the way they were. She had simply said there are certain things we are not meant to understand; we just have to accept them as God's will. She was not avoiding the questions, though who could have blamed her, this was simply the accepted philosophy of the day. You did not question God. I find it amazing how many still believe that. I was pleased to know that questions were neither forbidden, nor considered impertinent to God and His world. Quite the contrary, I have always found that they eagerly encouraged inquiries. They continued.

"We are all teachers, just as we are all students. There is always someone below you as well as above you on the path. We all become teachers by sharing our experiences and the wisdom which we have attained with others. We teach by example. All are capable of assisting and learning in some small measure.

"Perfecting the ability to love is an ever present need. One must learn to both give and accept love with equal grace. For, one is as important as the other. Some find giving love more comfortable while others are better able to accept love. When you can attain a perfect balance within these boundaries, then you will accept your brothers as they are without reservation. By the giving and receiving of love you share all that you are with another and in return accept all that they are. Offer your service and give of yourself freely, lovingly, asking nothing in return but the joy of the gift. Seek perfect balance in perfect love. Regardless of your level or world, the quest is the same. The only variation of the evolutionary process within the Father's world and all other worlds is the limitless possibilities available in attaining your goal. If one can not understand the importance of love, then he can not appreciate the importance of oneness with the Father, for the Father is love itself.

"At times it is difficult for some within your plane to understand that they are being taught. They do not consider that the everyday events which occur within their lives are a means of teaching. The stumbling blocks and difficulties you face temper the soul and make it strong. Encounters with other beings within your plane are never coincidental, but are always designed to teach. Everything within your plane or within any of the other worlds which the Father has created is designed for the advancement of the soul. That is the reason for your presence here. You are not here to mark time, nor to simply take up space. You are here to learn, to experience, and to love. All is carefully laid out and planned by a wisdom far greater than you can conceive. Paths are carefully intertwined so that the contact of every single solitary entity who enters your line of vision has a purpose. Nothing is left to chance. The more enlightened beings are allowed to draw to themselves the needed lessons and opportunities because they are considered wise enough to understand that these lessons, no matter how difficult, lift the soul. The obstacles encourage you to reach out for your Father. The roads you travel, the places you live, the beings which you encounter and the circumstances surrounding the encounters, the departures and separations within your life, all offer instruction. Your environment, you life's work, the knowledge you possess or the lack thereof, how you use that which is given, the love which you express to others, the circumstances which force you to reach out, all of these are a part of the plan. Situations along one's path are inserted at intervals in the hope that they will accomplish certain reactions.

"There are no words to describe the perfect love, beauty, and wisdom which lie within the Father, and were we able to explain, you would not understand. Your finite mind can not grasp the intricacies which lie within a being as omnipotent and a world as infinite as the Father's. He is all that is and ever shall be. All life contains the Father and were He not within it there would be no life. No matter how minute or lifeless an organism or object may seem, it can not survive without the Father in it. Without the Father there is no life and where God is not there is nothingness. We realize that this is difficult for you to conceive, for there are many things that are alive which you do not consider to be so. Everything that you can conceive, see, or reach out and touch lives, because the mind of the Father gives it life. Were life not present then an object simply would not exist. Everything you see within your plane is an illusory thought form which is created for your use. Understanding the concept of nothingness is difficult for you. You can not understand the absence of God. He is always there and those who declare they do not believe in His existence are foolish. If He did not exist, they would not exist, nor anything they see. Were He to withdraw from them, they would cease to be. He is in everyone and everything. Where there is life, if there is something, then the Father is present."

I wondered why we were here. I understand that we are here to learn, but it seemed as though we are incorrigible and I wondered if we had been created for a specific purpose or were we kind of an "Oops"? I guess I was really wondering if this arrangement was of any benefit to God? Were we of any use to Him or was He just patiently tolerating us?

"The Father created the souls so that they might jointly experiment and develop aspects of the worlds which he had produced. The souls were intended to be companions, aspects of Himself who could be sent out to experiment with various concepts. The worlds created by God are many and diverse. Each offers within it the opportunity to experience different things. The souls were meant to help to more fully experience the intricacies of being. They were intended to help in the creation of these worlds, thus, fulfilling their potential. Certain souls were designated to occupy a particular world and were then allowed to assist in the creation of the possibilities which would exist within each. Most of the souls complied and patiently awaited the necessary preparation and time of entry. The small planet Terra was unique, however. It was a planet created so that the Father might explore the effects of deception and illusion upon the soul. The intent was that a soul would learn to circumvent the illusions while maintaining its natural equilibrium. The souls designated to enter this planet became impatient. They began to hover too closely around this treacherous little world before they could be adequately prepared and became drawn into it.

"As any child within your plane carries the genetic make up of its parent, so the souls carry within them the genetic image of their Father. You are the higher echelon of His creations. You alone possess the reasoning powers to direct the other life-forms within the Earth. You hold sway over the animal, vegetable, and mineral kingdoms. Only the souls were given the ability to be co-creators with the Father. No other aspect of your world has this power. It is a gift which marks you as a child of God. You are able to create with your thoughts just as the Father does, and while your world draws an illusory cloak around that creative process, it is there nonetheless. Other worlds are more aware of their creativity and so have more control over these abilities. The nature of your plane, however, deceives you into believing that the things of your world are placed there by some means other than your own thought process. Your thought patterns and attitudes completely control your environment. You are unaware of this aspect of your being and make things more difficult than they need be. You flail, beat your chest, and cry out, asking the Father why He has placed you in such dire straits and why life is so cruel. My children, your surroundings are reflective of your feelings about them and will change accordingly. A situation and its compatibility to your life force is controlled by your attitude toward it. If you desire changes, then manifest them with your thoughts. The way to change things is by changing the way you think about them. The more attention you give to something the stronger it becomes. You give power to the negative aspects of your life by dwelling on them excessively. They feed on your despair. Accepting them gracefully as a natural part of your lessons, will make them less prevalent. Remember, only you among the Father's creatures have the power to create your environment. The rocks do not, they lay where they are placed. The flowers grow where there is enough water and sunshine to make them flourish. Animals are dependent either upon man or their natural environment and their ability to hunt for food. You, my children, are dependent solely upon yourselves and your Father. You are unique in this respect. Do you remember when the Master spoke to you saying, 'if you say to this mountain move from here to there, and believe, it will be so.' Ponder this. Think on what He truly meant. He was referring to your ability to control your habitat with your thought patterns.

"Man thinks the Father to be some distant personage in a far away secluded place who occasionally glances down upon His children to direct the occurrences which are to difficult for them to manage. They see Him as a being who dispenses punishment for wrong doing and little-known reasons which they are not meant to understand. They consider that He tests their strength and loyalty, expecting them to accept their lot in life without question. His power and omnipotence they understand, though their concept is extremely limited. That one so omnipotent and powerful could be a part of their being, remaining lovingly within is beyond their comprehension. They do not recognize the love of their Father because they do not understand that real love and power are synonymous. You have allowed this dark place to play tricks with your mind. Unable to love yourselves, you can not understand how God can love you. Thus, you believe that He takes no notice of you except to punish and take those you love from you. Memory of life beyond this world is obscured and you can not envision any existence other than the familiar little prison which you occupy. This cramped and painful existence you believe to be life. You view the dark little world which you inhabit as a place of life and beauty. Oh, my children, this is not life. Life awaits you. Life is free, loving, beautiful, joyous, and patient. We had so hoped that you would realize that your stay within the body is merely a lesson. If you accept life within the Earth plane as the ultimate, then you set your standards far too low. you can not understand your Father because you can not comprehend life, love, freedom, and beauty. God embodies all these attributes. In your suffering you say to yourself, it is God's will. My dear children, God does not will you to suffer. You choose your own suffering. Take the responsibility for your own actions. Do not lay at the Father's door the blame for what you created. Expecting someone else to shoulder your responsibilities has been one of your problems from the beginning. Your pain is completely unnecessary. His only wish for you is that you allow Him to love you, allow your brothers to love you, and for you to love them in return. In order to understand God you must understand love. Love holds within it no punishment or recrimination. Love knows nothing of anger, hatred, and does not keep lists of rights and wrongs. Love is gentle, patient, compassionate, accepting, and non judgmental."

When we first began the sessions many of the questions we asked had to do with how we could change or create a desired result. The answer invariably came back, "Be more loving." We would sigh and phrase the question differently hoping for a more specific answer. The answer, however, was always the same, If you want things to turn out better or differently then approach them with a more loving attitude. It is so easy to off-handedly dismiss or overlook this concept as too simple. It leaves no room, however, for a common knee-jerk reaction to situations and the behavior of others. You must teach yourself to be thoughtful and sensitive, rather than just reacting. If you can master it, it does work! They resumed.

"With the acceptance of love, comes understanding. Learn to understand the vastness of God's creations and the link which binds them all together. You need not complicate the lesson with rules and lists of rights and wrongs, do's and don'ts. Learn only one thing, to love. Knock down the barriers and walls, Unlock the doors, swing them wide and let the love in. It banishes the darkness. Suddenly, all the things which have been obscured from your vision are clear. Reach out to others in love and accept the love which they offer and all things will become new again. Depravity can not survive in the light. The light brings with it understanding of the little demons which hide in the dark corners.

"If you would but allow your mind to float freely you could escape the rigidity of illusory concepts. The unrelenting assumption of logic prevents you from opening to the divergent possibilities and the limitlessness of the Father's world. Allow yourself to open and expand outward, reaching beyond the fallacy which traps you. Clear away the mists and fog so that you may see clearly the reality which lies beyond. You can not do this, however, as long as you place so much emphasis on the petty little restrictions and lists which hold you and keep you from loving your brother. The key to opening your heart is to simply reach out in love. One's race, creed, gender, social standing, achievements, or religious affiliation are irrelevant. These are things of the body, illusions which dissolve when the soul departs. There is little more than a veil which distorts your vision. All souls underneath the facade of the body are the same. You must not allow the body to keep you from your task or keep you from discovering the beauty of love. You must not allow yourself to be bogged down by the pettiness of your world. Learn to see with your heart instead of your eyes. Let love lead the way. Reach out in love to your brothers, ignoring what you see on the outside. It is only a costume, a temporary disguise. Release your mind and heart from the confines and logic of this plane. Let it fly freely upward toward the Father. Do not weigh it down with inconsequential matters which only serve greed and power. Open your mind, heart, and spirit to the possibilities within, allowing them to become limitless. Love is sufficient unto itself!

"For man to experience the vast limitlessness of the Father's kingdom within the three dimensional state, he must look within. Outside the body all is illusory, limited, weighed down, and darkened by the qualities of your plane. It all seems so real to you, but then have you not had vivid dreams, remarking to yourself how closely they paralleled reality? We are trying to explain to you, my children, that your plane resembles the dream state. you give your plane more credence, when actually the dream state is more credible than the world around you. Dreams come from within your being. They are staged, written, and cast by you as a problem solving tool. Within the dream state you are absolutely unlimited. You can do things, go places and be individuals which are no possible within the body. Yet you consider the body and the plane you occupy the reality and the dream state an illusion. You have it backward. The door which leads to the limitless reality of your Father's kingdom can only be reached from within. What lies outside your being is not reality and is of little use to you other than to help you to focus more intently on a lesson. With a great deal of study you can open your mind to the reality within. Only this will offer you the freedom and sustenance your soul craves so desperately. Only the offering of unselfish love can release the door."

CHAPTER XII

THE MESSENGERS

I wish I could give you the names of the beings who spoke with me, but none were ever given. When I asked, they countered that names were unimportant and was not the means by which they identified another. It was the message, they assured me, not the messenger which was important. They did, however, explain much about themselves and their mission both here and within the Father's world.

"We are members of a brotherhood called Raphael which was established aeons ago. We are the Children of Light and asked the Father if we might intercede on behalf of those entangled within your plane. Many representatives of our brotherhood have spoken with man through the ages, using philosophy, religion, poetry, music, art, literature, and all manner of communication. Regardless of the manner and eloquence of our communication, man invariably twists our words, discounts their source, mistrusts our motives, or attributes our communication to superstition, or demons. You are difficult to reach. Attempts have been made to approach you on all levels of your society. You have been approached physically, intellectually, and emotionally, though the latter is a particularly difficult avenue for us, as it fluctuates far too much and tends toward instability. It lacks the enduring effects which our purposes require. Our brotherhood seeks more the communication of the mind, for we bring the light which is the mind of God.

"Our brotherhood originally consisted of twenty-five select beings who agreed to share the light within them with you. Each of these twenty-five souls has many different facets who work within your plane, attempting to infiltrate the brotherhood of man. It is necessary that a portion of our brotherhood be within the body while the others remain within the Father's world.

Those within God's kingdom transfer information which they possess or gather from the Elders and Wise Ones to those of our number who are incarnate at that time. This occurs within many worlds, but none quite so intently as within the Earth plane. The very nature of your environment complicates and limits the thinking process more than in other worlds. Your plane is the only one in which a being does not have full access to his subconscious mind, creating difficulties not present within other planes. Your environment absorbs knowledge, inviting you to forget. Those of our brotherhood who enter are subliminally programmed through the stages of growth until they have reached the agreed upon time of awakening to the knowledge within them. Often, only a portion of a soul descends into a single body. It is easier to reach man in this manner. The portion of their 'oversoul' remaining within the Father's world facilitates communication. The messages are brought in this manner. A communication link is established, forming a triangle of light. The pinnacle of the triangle is the Father, the source of the light. His light is projected to the communicator, who in turn passes it to the receptor to convey to man in whatever manner he sees fit. Thus, the wisdom of the Father is carried in many ways into your plane."

I was stunned. I had just been told, indirectly, that I was a receptor for information from a group of enlightened beings. At first I was terribly frightened. This differed from everything I had ever been taught. How could I tell anyone? They would laugh in my face. The conveyor did not seem at all concerned with the reaction of others, nor my fears of being a social outcast. They informed me that I had agreed to do this before entering the body and had been prepared my whole life to disregard the judgment of others and respond only to the Father's voice. They assured me there was no need for concern, all that I needed would be provided.

"Our brotherhood increases as evidence of the evolutionary level of man rises toward enlightenment. As one reaches the pinnacle of enlightenment he feels compelled to serve. Each time a child of God reaches that pinnacle he is allowed to choose the particular form of service he will enter. Ours is a teaching brotherhood. We bring knowledge of the light; how to accept it into your being and absorb from it the wisdom of the ages. All our members are teachers in one form or another. Our manner of education varies depending upon the individual needs and abilities of a soul. When one reaches a state of enlightenment, it is assumed that he will use his gifts in some form of service to others and is deemed wise enough to choose for himself the form his service will take. Teaching is only one. There are many others. One can always attain new growth, either within our brotherhood or another still more exalted one. Here you are measured by no yardstick other than your capacity to love. We share all that we are with others. Competition is not necessary. For what would we compete? There is no need for wealth or prestige here. Prestige is gained through one's ability to love. There is no need to compete for power or position, Love is all powerful. Competition for the Father's love is unnecessary, for we each have it in great abundance. There is no false modesty here. One performs according to his capabilities. Accomplishments are evident in the radiance of one's light."

I had not heard of heavenly brotherhoods before and was interested to learn more about them. What was their function? How did one become a part of a brotherhood? Were there many and did each one have a different function? They answered my questions candidly and gladly, as always.

"Certain criterion are required for membership in our brotherhood. The primary standard, obviously, must be enlightenment. Only with enlightenment does one acquire the true desire for service and the selfless need to share with others knowledge of the Father. With enlightenment one gains the wisdom and understanding which enables him to share the light, while allowing another the freedom to choose for himself. It is not an easy task and man does not always respond lovingly. It is felt, however, that only those who have attained an enlightened state can accomplish this without being discouraged or having their beliefs damaged. Not all accept our message favorably, yet we must approach them with patience and love all the same. If we can communicate with them in no other way, we must convey our convictions by the example of our being. They must see the Father reflected within us and if possible, we share with them the knowledge which we possess of His kingdom. Prudence is of the essence, one must never force himself upon another. It takes great strength to approach others and not be discouraged by their anger, skepticism, ridicule or any other form their unbelief takes. These things are required, a patient soul, a loving heart, an enlightened being, and a willingness to share all that you know, are, and have ever been with your brothers.

"We approach man with our knowledge from many different directions, both consciously and subliminally. We use every means and method available to us to attain this end. It is often a subtle process. We try, in some small measure, to remove man's aggressive tendencies. If we can replace his quick anger with a willingness to reach out to his brothers in understanding and love, then a phenomenal change will occur. We shall attempt to encourage him to look within if only briefly and see the light nestled there. Recognition of the light will fan the flame of his being higher, hastening his upward momentum. If man wishes to reach what lies beyond his prison, then we can assist him. Until he realizes, however, that reality lies beyond his present condition here, there is little we can do.

"There are many ways of reaching another. Not all are verbal. We are experimenting with many different methods. Each being, no matter how closed minded he is, or impossible he may seem shall have the opportunity to be one with the light. All God's children possess His light within. Our goal is to help them to understand and seek that light. If the search consists of only a glance in the right direction, it is enough. Often you are not aware of the affect you have upon those you encounter. So, take great care to always express the love and beauty within your being. Allow it to shine through, for you never know who is watching or how seeing your smile and the glow of love within your face may affect them.

"Within the Father's world the brotherhoods exist to fulfill the need for service. Unlike your plane, we have no need for leisure or amusement. We do not require sleep, relaxation, or any of the things which you employ to amuse yourselves in order to alleviate the stress of your existence. We find joy in our work, for our work is always about the business of love. Each entity within the Father's world performs some service, not because they are forced to, but because they choose to. Offering love resembles throwing a pebble into a pond. When the pebble strikes the water it creates ripples which reverberate outward from the origin. Love is never shared with just one, but is given to many. When another is drawn into the circle of love all benefit, for the light increases."

They had mentioned the term *oversoul* which was new to me. I was curious about how an oversoul differed from any other soul.

"Each soul has many facets within itself, just as an entity within the body has many talents and personality traits incorporated within the whole. Often only a fragment or facet of the entire soul is sent into the body. Sending a fragment in no way weakens a soul, nor does it make it less effective. Each has at its command all the power, knowledge, and talents contained within the whole. Knowledge of and wisdom possessed by the whole is accessible through the subconscious mind. So, while there are only twenty-five oversouls within our particular brotherhood, each of those souls has many, many facets which can be used to project itself. When an aspect leaves the body it rejoins the oversoul, incorporating into it the wisdom which has been acquired. We realize this concept may, perhaps, be difficult for you, but as you evolve your understanding will grow. Each of you is a part of an extraordinarily powerful soul and use only a fraction of the power available to you."

I am still not certain that I completely understand the concept of only a facet of a soul being used within a single body to experience a particular aspect of life. My finite mind has difficulty understanding how there can be so many separate individuals within one soul. No matter how many times they explained or how many different approaches they used I still had difficulty grasping it. They calmly reminded me that I should not distress myself unduly and assured me that in time I would understand. I wanted to know more about enlightenment. I found that many of my concepts about how one became enlightened and how to distinguish them from others were not completely accurate.

"When one reaches the state of enlightenment he does not consider only what benefits himself, but how he may best serve the common good of all. He understands that love and satisfaction are received automatically with service to others.

Recognition and reward do not concern him. Service and love consume him, for he knows of no other way in which to express his being. The higher forms of service do not require one to enter the body unless he chooses to. An enlightened being radiates light, not only from the area of the mind, but throughout his entire being. It infuses every cell of his being. When one is less enlightened the light is present, but buried deeply within his mind. The farther out the light radiates from the mind, the more enlightened, or the closer to enlightenment an individual is. We are able to see the light within one who occupies a body and discern the distance of its radiation from the mind. Thus we are able to perceive one's potential for enlightenment. Such beings will be more receptive to our approach and possess the ability to respond to the call of the light."

When we were first told of their ability to discern enlighten-ment within an individual we began asking about many of our acquaintances. We were often surprised by their replies and found many whom we did not suspect. I guess that proves the old adage, "You can't judge a book by its cover." They continued by cautioning us not to use enlightenment as a status symbol.

"Each and every one will be allowed to accept or reject the light. Those who accept will be brought upward on the evolu-tionary scale one step at a time as they are able. They will be allowed whatever time is necessary to absorb and complete the levels which they lack. Ways of service which advance one more rapidly and aid in gaining the next level will be offered. In becoming a part of the Father, we become one with all that is. The need for recycling, rejuvenating, and reeducating will have ceased. The glorious beauty of His love will be realized and there will be no more fragments, divisions, or separations.

"A great many of our brothers live within your world in different locations. They possess varied levels of intelligence, race, and social circumstances, but they all carry within them the power of the light. Each is being awakened at a different time and location in response to their own prearranged cues. The awakenings will occur at a time which is most beneficial to their purposes. You will learn to recognize one another, using your mind. In your communion you will acquire a strength of pur-pose which can not be overrun by any power contrived by man.

"We seek the attention of man at this time because he has reached a point in his evolution at which he is in danger of standing still. The things he considers important have begun to crumble. The religious beliefs which have sustained him no longer fill his needs. The spiritual sustenance which his soul desired deep within seems remote and inaccessible. The religious organizations of today are obsessed with the material aspects of being rather than the Father's love. Man does not know where to find what he needs. Feeling as though these values were present in the past, he tries to recapture it. The past, however, can never be recaptured and indeed, should not be. One must go forward, never digressing, always climbing ever upward on the ladder toward the Father. Man stands at a cross roads. Confronted with two paths, he does not know which to take. His religion tells him of ways in which he may acquire spiritual enlightenment, but deep within he senses that something very subtle is lacking. Great strides have been made in acquiring scientific knowledge. He has overcome the elements and illness of his world and gained a great deal materially, yet, it brings him no comfort. He is filled with a gnawing ache which knows there must be more. The peace and joy promised by the religions of the world has not come to pass. The material possessions are hollow and bring only momentary respite. When one comes to understand the emptiness of seeking the material, we can approach him, encouraging him to reach upward toward the Father. If he can turn toward the light, or come into the light with us, then he may know his true self."

They were gentle and loving in their explanations but pulled no punches about the consequences of refusal to accept the path of love and light.

"In knowing, you shall find the joy, love, and peace which your soul so desperately seeks. You must choose. You may lift yourself into the light or deteriorate and stagnate back into nothingness. If you choose the latter, then you must begin again, struggling along the long path back to the Father. It will be a difficult climb, for those who chose the light will carry the love with them, leaving you to struggle through the debris of your own depravity. If you can not or do not wish to climb back up again you will simply cease to be. We speak with you now in an effort to encourage you toward love and the light. If one desires union with the Father and possesses the patience and diligence to acquire it, then it shall be his. Within the Father's kingdom all things are possible for he who loves.

"God honors all brotherhoods and their service. He is pleased by any act which originates in love, regardless of how menial you may consider it to be. None is too insignificant for the Father's notice. A loving heart can not fail to influence those who are a party to its offerings. Can there be a purer love than the love of a small child not yet old enough to realize that he deserves to be loved in return? Even the lowliest animal asks nothing of you but your caring, offering in return their unconditional devotion. There is no more precious gift in all the Father's kingdom, yeah, in all of infinity than the gift of love. Whatever else he may be, if a soul can offer love to another, regardless of how limited, the Father will never abandon him. Where there is love there is hope. We and all brotherhoods within God's kingdom serve a code of conduct whose origin is love. There is no other. All we do, are, and hope to be is born of love. Everything begins and ends in love. The stepping stones which enable you to climb upward are formed by love. There is no other path by which you may find God. You can make no bargains, nor negotiate any tradeoffs. You are judged by only one thing, your capacity to love. Remember, within the Father's kingdom you do not have the power to deceive. You no longer have the facade of the body with which to disguise your inability to love. When you withhold love or fail to recognize its importance, then you do harm to no one but yourself. You must learn the true meaning of love. It is not simply giving another everything he wants. Do not confuse love with indulgence. Real love is being sensitive enough to understand another's needs, which do not always coincide with his wants. We do not speak of material things, for there is nothing within the Father's world which has to do with the material. The gift you give to another which is of the most value is the love within your heart. The radiance of love transcends all barriers and all worlds in its clear, bright, beautiful truth. We are drawn to those who manifest the light and can not resist the love which motivates a call to help another. That which is requested from a loving heart is provided.

"An individual may use his own discretion in accepting or rejecting our offer of assistance. Some never find the quiet place within, or completely bring contact with the brotherhood into their conscious mind. They are only aware that certain things inspire them to better things, make them euphoric, or give them a sense of peace and well-being. Anyone who feels love and compassion for others is in contact with a brotherhood, whether he is aware of it or not. Some brotherhoods take a more highly evolved form than others. Not all beings are able to handle the more highly evolved communications, however, and are given what their abilities dictate. Great responsibility accompanies the relaying of knowledge. The Father does not entrust the ability casually, nor does He entrust it to those He feels are incapable of handling it wisely."

I wondered if everyone within the Father's world is a part of a brotherhood? What about those to whom they minister within the Earth plane, are they all members of a brotherhood? As we went along I found that the one constant was the increasing number of questions which filled my mind. They patiently explained and answered my queries, sometimes repeatedly.

"Not everyone within the Earth plane belongs to a brotherhood. All have the option and there are brotherhoods who nurture even those who seem unworthy of even the smallest loving kindness. Often these need nurturing most. Some do not seem motivated by anything other than the very lowest elements. It is possible, however, for the Father and some of His messengers to reach even these. If a being has a need for sustenance, regardless of how small, then one of the brotherhoods will provide what is needed. All are reachable. All, however, do not choose to be reached. Some choose to turn their back on love and those who offer it. This is their right. The door is never closed and the offer never withdrawn even though one continually rejects all overtures. No one is ever shut out or ignored or turned away without recourse. If one reaches out to another in love, regardless of how fleeting the gesture, it does not go unnoticed. Each spark of love is nurtured and encouraged in the hope that it will increase. The choice is yours. We will not force our help upon you.

"The members of all the brotherhoods working from within the Father's world are enlightened beings. The beings who occupy the Earth plane are not necessarily. Those who are influenced more by the senses are not always enlightened. With enlightenment one acquires the wisdom needed to use their influence wisely. We who serve the Father do not seek to manipulate man in any way. When the five senses are used to reach man, we use the utmost discretion and wisdom so as to avoid any hint of trickery or exploitation. Your plane has far too much of that already. We simply inspire you in the hope that you will seek the source of that inspiration. Our brotherhood encourages a higher sense. The sixth sense, which is simply a seemingly inexplicable knowledge of the truth. Our contact is made through a more direct mental channel. Therefore, our subjects within the Earth plane must be very enlightened to understand the truth which comes through them. All beings have the potential for enlightenment and come a step closer to it each time they enter the school room of the body."

When I was a child, attending church in the bible belt south, we were always cautioned that man sat on the precipice of doom and that the destruction of his world and life as we know it was an ever present danger. Dire warnings of this eminent peril were used by many a minister to strike fear in the hearts of his followers and to encourage them toward a more Godly existence. Since the time of Christ there has been continuous speculation about when this apocalypse would occur. I inquired about these doomsday predictions and asked them to comment.

"The momentum of evolution carries all upward in its wake. Regardless of the time required, all shall be one with our Father again. As long as you struggle with your world, seeking to rise above it, we shall assist you. For, until all are free, none can be free. A specific timetable as you calculate years, months, or days does not exist for accomplishing our goal. We do not use time as you do. Within our world there is no time, there are only opportunities for growth, love, and the potential for learning. When each is able to accept fully the opportunities for love available to him at this level, then he will automatically be lifted upward along with those of the same capabilities. You have not reached the archetype of evolution simply because you have made technological or scientific advances which preserve the body for longer periods. The ability to sustain life is given from God and is not within the power of your world. Upon departure from the body you will see the foolishness of agonizing over the material aspects of your plane. The more you learn to love and forgive, the more rapidly you will advance on the evolutionary ladder. It is these abilities which give you momentum.

"There are many of us among you. We assist however we may. We do not force, nor make choices for another. We offer love and light and allow others to choose how they will use the gifts. Many inquire, upon encountering one of our brotherhood, about the source of his information. There is but one source and that is the mind of God. There are those close to Him who are better able to understand the knowledge, and wise enough to commune with Him. These Wise Ones and Elders relay their communication to we who serve Him. There are many messengers, but only one source."

I was concerned about how to approach others with the knowledge I was being given. I have always possessed some rather unconventional ideas and have been the recipient of more than one baffled look and shaken head. I did not want this wisdom to be dismissed as the ravings of some eccentric weirdo. I wanted others to recognize its spark of light and truth and seek more. I was aware that it would be difficult for others to believe that I had been graced with the conveying of such wisdom. I had difficulty believing it myself. How then could I approach them so that they would listen and think, rather than simply dismissing me as just another flake? They, as always, were eager to help and found none of my questions to trivial for answers.

"Those who are unaware of our existence may be reached simply by our presence among them. Allowing them to see our attitudes and the way in which we conduct our lives will encourage their aspirations to behave in like manner. If you are asked how you find the courage to face the difficulties of this life with such grace, you may instruct on whatever level the questioner is able to understand. If one is able to ask, then they are able to understand. Some are unable to grasp the finer points at first, but the seeds which will eventually blossom within their minds may be sown. The greatest teacher, however, is the way in which you conduct your own life. Your resistance to anger will help to dissuade others from their anger. Observing your behavior will influence others more than any other single thing. When they seek to acquire like responses, then you may begin to instruct, encouraging them to reach out. Grace and patience are the most profound instruments of teaching. If one is affected even for a brief moment, it will be one less moment in which they have exercised anger and the lower elements of the personality. If these moments can be strung together, then they can perhaps be retained for longer periods of time. Out of small victories come larger ones. Do not be disappointed that everyone does not understand immediately. Everyone does not grow at the same pace. If they grow at all it is a victory and carries within it the possibility of more.

"The methods by which we accomplish our goals must be geared to those whom we are with at the time and the level on which they respond. Some may be influenced by the love, gentleness, and kind attention projected to them, others by a simple smile. Some will reach out to an attitude which you project. They will seek your presence because it is cheerful, warm, and loving. They feel at peace and a sense of harmony within themselves when you are there. Some may understand your teachings, or you may adapt the knowledge to their level of understanding. Others respond to higher aspirations and can begin work on the more esoteric levels of information, then there are those who simply need awakening. There are many who, while not enlightened, are capable of understanding many things included within the higher knowledge. Use whatever means you feel appropriate for a particular individual or group. Often your presence and the love you project will suffice. Many are receptive to subliminal suggestion without realizing it consciously. Care must be taken, however, that messages sent subliminally are of love and beauty and not designed in any way to manipulate. All must be allowed to choose freely. If their choice is not freely made, then it is your choice not theirs. Remember at all times not to suppress another's own individual beauty, creativity, and right of choice. This is our most important directive. We may give love, encouragement, and patience, but we may never coerce. We may offer the light, but we may never force the taking of the light upon another.

"The end result will lift mankind to his highest potential on whatever level or dimension he occupies. This does no necessarily mean that all will be on the same tier. The need to traverse many levels and dimensions will remain. We wish for man to be the very best that he can be. Our mission at this time is to use all the resources available to us to lift man toward the very pinnacle of his potential on whatever plane he occupies. This specific phase has accomplished all that is possible at this time. If man is to go upward then he must reach for the next step. The supreme attainments in evolution are within one's mind and attitudes toward others. Spirituality of the mind and soul must evolve. Man has not even begun to scratch the surface in this area. You need to understand that you must reach beyond the physical, beyond the technology and the scientifically arrogant bravado around you. The real challenge lies within and you must seek that reality.

"When an evolutionary step is indicated, our brotherhood is sent to approach man in this manner. When there is the possibility that he can accept newer broader concepts, we approach, encouraging the opening of his consciousness to the realities which lie beyond. If you can free your mind and allow it to drift upward, circumventing the limited concepts of your world, then you can accept the true reality. If one has attained all that is attainable within your world and still finds no satisfaction or deep meaning within his existence there, then he must seek elsewhere. When enough reach out, seeking the true reality, we approach, offering the light. This is not the first time the light has been offered, nor shall it be the last."

I remembered the passage in the bible when Jesus had been brought before the Sanhedrin and was asked by whose authority He spoke. I knew who was speaking to me I could feel it in my soul, but I knew that inevitably this question would come up. So I ask of them how I should respond.

"We know that our path is the correct one because the Father has said that it is so. He is all-knowing, all-loving, and omnipotent. He alone knows the path which will offer the opportunities to advance the evolution of the soul. Only the Father is wise enough to correlate all patterns of growth within Himself and disperse just the right one to each individual soul so that he may

experience the growth which is most advantageous. There is only
one way to the Father and that is through love. There can be no
question as to right or wrong. One either loves or he does not. If
one loves, then he advances along the path, regardless of the
speed of that advancement. If he can not love then there is little
left for him and no point to his existence. There need be no
confusion about goals, destinies, or means of achieving these.
There is but one goal and that is to be one with the Father. There
is but one means of achieving that goal and that is through love.
One must love simply because it is the only acceptable behavior
for a child of our Holy Father. The light with which we have
been entrusted contains the wisdom through which we gain
access to the truth. No one has the ability to supersede the
Father and insert his own truth. You can trust that the light
which we offer will enable the love and wisdom of the Father to
rest within the heart of each of you. By examining it and learning
to love without condition, you will know the truth contained
within. The Father will allow no trickster to intervene and
deceive you, concerning the light. If the message is one of love,
gentleness, kindness, compassion, and joy then it is truth regardless of its messenger. You may judge the truth of a teaching by
the love contained within it. There will be no malice, hatred,
anger, or pettiness, yeah, not even a hint of it. There will be only
the purest radiant love, undiminished in its glory. Anyone who
offers you anything else, or attempts to force you in any way was
not sent by the Father. Any choice or love submitted out of fear
is meaningless. Love can only be offered from a loving joyful
heart, spontaneously given without coercion. The truth of our
claims is substantiated by the Father and the love which emanates from our message.

"All the power and beauty contained within the light is at
your command. God does not entrust His sacred light to those
who are careless with it. He knows the intentions of your mind
and the yearnings of your heart. For this reason He selects only
those whose motives are sincere and those who possess the
strength and courage to impart His light. As the Master said, 'You
do not throw pearls before swine.' Only those who are capable of
nurturing and understanding the true meaning of the light are
entrusted with a gift so precious. Only the Father sees you as you
truly are within. He alone chooses those He will send and those

with whom we are speaking have been chosen for this task. It has been our mission from the beginning of time to bring the light of the Father into all the dark recesses of infinity, illuminating all that is with the wisdom, beauty, and love which emanates from our Holy Father, God.

He has been called Jehovah, Yahweh, Emanuel, Jesus, Holiest of Holies, Our Father, God, Love, Beauty, and The Light. All flow from His holy presence. Wisdom flows from His being through the Elders, Wise Ones, and we His humblest servants. He is the source of all that is and ever shall be. He is our Father and our God and our Christ. We are privileged and honored to be allowed to reflect His light. We are humbled by His trust and the light entrusted to us. His name is so glorious that the hearing of it is painful to the ear. You have but to listen to the quiet recesses of your mind and contemplate the warmth within your heart. His name, my beloved child, is love. When you understand, then you will know that this is the only name glorious enough to befit one so Holy as He. Amen and Amen."

"So my child, if there is no death,
and I assure you there is not;
why do you tremble before
your nameless phantoms?

What is it you fear?
Life? Love? Light?
You allow yourself to be
haunted needlessly.

For, my beloved child,
there is only you and I
and the love, laughter, and
life that we share.

The only devil is the
fear which separates us."

P.J.I. (10/12/87)

ABOUT THE AUTHOR

Patricia Idol considers herself a "career" mother who enjoys her work. She has been happily married to the same man for 37 years. She has two surviving grown children, three grandsons, (four if you include her daughter's Lhasa Apso, Sydney).

As early as her teens, she began writing as a cathartic exercise, in part to express some of the aspects of her life which she did not feel comfortable discussing with others. Although she kept files and journals for many years, it was not until two years after her son's death that the revelations began and thoughts flowed effortlessly in a steady unbroken stream—as though they were waiting for the appointed time.

Pat quotes the *Egyptian Book of the Dead*: "On my heart I bear the scars to prove that I have lived." She goes on to say:

"I believe in miracles! I have experienced too many to ignore them. I also know, however, that what seems to be a miracle in our Earthly dimension is only the manifestation of events already laid out by wiser sources."